SESSIONS WITH REVELATION

Smyth & Helwys Publishing, Inc.
6316 Peake Road
Macon, Georgia 31210-3960
1-800-747-3016
© 2014 by Smyth & Helwys Publishing
All rights reserved.

Library of Congress Cataloging-in-Publication Data

Sapp, David.
Sessions with Revelation : the last days of evil / by David Sapp.
pages cm
Includes bibliographical references.
ISBN 978-1-57312-706-6 (pbk. : alk. paper)
1. Bible. Revelation--Commentaries. I. Title.
BS2825.53.S27 2014
228'.07--dc23

2013047745

Sessions *with*
• Revelation

The *Last Days* of *Evil*

David Sapp

SMYTH&HELWYS
PUBLISHING INCORPORATED   MACON GEORGIA
WWW.HELWYS.COM

For Linda, Benjamin, and Matthew
who have been for me a revelation of God's love

Acknowledgments

No book can be written by an author alone. The distinguishing feature of this book, however, is that it is more dependent on others who have influenced the author than any other book ever written. I am quite sure of this. This writing has been a community project, really, and has been contributed to by legions of people who have been a part of my life. Let me try to name just a few members of this deeply appreciated group.

First of all, some pastors and Sunday School teachers of my youth stimulated my original interest in the book of Revelation. Then, when I arrived at Mercer University as a freshman, my faculty advisor, Ray Brewster, invited me to help him start a 7:00 a.m. Bible study with several of my friends. For that entire year, we studied Revelation with early morning adolescent foggy mindedness, but had our eyes opened to that fact that Revelation was far more than the handbook for the end times we had to that point understood it to be.

I also began in those years to be interested in writing. Foy Valentine, the late, great Baptist ethicist who was both my mentor and my tormentor, taught me more than anyone else about writing. He wrote with forceful clarity, and while he never was able to teach me to write as he did, he did help me write with less unclarity than I had ever done before.

I also owe a lot to many friends who have encouraged me to write. These include people like Foy Valentine, Bill Hull, Peter Rhea Jones, David Currie, Floyd Craig, Charles Qualls, Timothy Norton, and others. The "others" know who they are. The confidence of this group has been a strong motivator for me to undertake this effort.

In addition, three great churches have allowed me to serve them as pastor since seminary. The people of these churches have listened patiently to my teaching on Revelation and have given honest feedback. Special thanks is due to the people of my last pastorate, the Second-Ponce de Leon Baptist Church of Atlanta. They gave me as much freedom to write as they could.

Finally, my family helped to write this book. Linda, my long-suffering wife, listened to most of this book as I read it aloud. Her many suggestions and reactions made my writing considerably lessened the obscurity of my writing. The obscurity that remains is all mine. She also did me the singular favor of relentlessly encouraging me to write. Our sons, Matthew and

Benjamin, have for many years been my most frequent—and often my most challenging— theological dialogue partners. I owe them more than I can say.

To all these, to others whose names I have overlooked, and to God, I give thanks.

Table of Contents

Introducing Revelation

My journey with Revelation began at an early age. Many of my friends were frightened by its images, but I was mesmerized by the preaching I heard from its strange-sounding texts. At first I took at face value the teaching about Revelation that I heard from the pulpit, but as I grew older, some of it didn't ring right even in my still-young ears.

I remember riding in the car one morning as Dad drove me to my summer job. I was watching the sunrise, and I tried to imagine the second coming. I squinted at the sky and did my best to picture Jesus breaking through the clouds in a blaze of light. I tried to imagine that blaze being visible all around the world, and I tried to visualize graves opening and the living and the dead floating up to meet Christ in the air. The night before, when I heard it preached at a revival, it had all seemed perfectly real. But now, in my adolescent sunrise sleepiness, it seemed somehow unreal, impossible, and regrettably unbelievable. How would this work so that people on all sides of the earth could see him at the same time? I knew that I believed, but this version of the second coming seemed too much like something out of a cheap novel. I knew I was supposed to believe it, and I was too timid to say it, but it just didn't feel right.

Ever since, I have struggled with Revelation. I have read it over and over, preached from it, and taught it on numerous occasions. As the pastor of the First Baptist Church of Chamblee, Georgia, during the 1980s, I decided to teach the book from the book itself. I chose not to read any interpretation but to do my best to grapple only with what the text said. I read Revelation through five times before I ever taught the first lesson, and I made an amazing discovery. Growing up, I had learned about many ideas that were supposed to be in Revelation. They are not in the book! There is no rapture, no seven-year tribulation, and no clear indication of whether John advocated pre-, post-, or amillenialism.

It took me a long time to come to grips with my discovery. I had thoroughly learned the lessons I was taught. I had been impressed with the deeply impassioned preaching I had heard. Besides, everybody believed in this interpretation of John's ancient book. I didn't know anyone—no Christians, anyway—who did not understand Revelation in the framework of those ideas. I discovered later that most of them had never actually read Revelation, at least not without the aid of an interpreter with charts and codes and strange linkages to other obscure Bible passages to justify his or her own particular interpretation.

Somewhere along the way, I began to ask questions. I started to wonder why it was so hard to find what I believed were the key teachings about Revelation in the text itself. I wondered why it was necessary to hop through the Bible, linking passages that didn't always seem to relate to each other, in order to understand God's scenario for the end times. If God wanted us to have this Revelation, I began to ask, why did God give it to us in hidden form that no one was able to decipher until the early 1800s, when the interpretation I grew up on was first devised? I could not understand why Revelation was not *revealing*.

I taught Revelation again years later when I served as pastor of the Derbyshire Baptist Church in Richmond, Virginia, and yet again when I served as pastor of the Second-Ponce de Leon Baptist Church in Atlanta, Georgia. Each time, I saw new layers in John's vision buried beneath the ones I had seen before. Finally, writing this book has provided the most recent occasion to delve more deeply into the Apocalypse (another name for Revelation). Each time I work my way through it, the book gets richer. Each time, it reveals more of its mysteries. Still, I must confess, it also raises new questions and presents new mysteries each time I read it.

I am by no means a scholarly specialist on Revelation, as any scholarly specialist who happens to read this book will quickly realize. I am a pastor. I understand this book as a pastor, as a letter received from heaven with a message for my church. But, come to think of it, this is exactly how Revelation was written in the first place. Maybe, as a pastor, I have a bit of an advantage in interpreting it. Maybe not. You decide. Meanwhile, I hope this study is helpful, takes you into new territory, and makes you think new thoughts about this book. If you conclude that my understanding makes sense, that will be great. If you conclude that I am totally wrong, that will be fine too. The church has survived for two thousand years while Christians have disagreed about the book of Revelation. It will survive if you and I do not agree. I do have one hope for this study that I hold sacred: I hope it will stimulate in you the kind of life-long curiosity about this book that will make you examine it again and again.

Before we plunge into our examination of this great Apocalypse, it will help to ask two questions: (1) Who wrote Revelation and when? (2) What kind of writing is it? Both questions will aid us in understanding what some regard as an incomprehensible book. Here is a brief discussion of each question.

Who Wrote Revelation and When?

An inexhaustible supply of scholarly debate swirls around who wrote Revelation and when that person wrote it. We will not spend much time on these questions here, but any serious reader of Revelation needs to think about them because they have the potential to affect how we understand the book.

The question of who wrote Revelation arises because the John who identifies himself as the author of Revelation does not tell us which John he is. Almost every John mentioned in the Bible or the early church has been suggested as the author at one time or another.

The earliest idea, and the one that is most common today, is that John the Apostle, the son of Zebedee, wrote Revelation. Although this is never stated in the book itself, the earliest scholars of the church believed he was the writer. By the mid-200s AD, however, some Christian thinkers began to have doubts. A man named Dionysius was bishop in Alexandria during this period, and many of his people became obsessed with millennial teachings. Dionysus began to pay careful attention to Revelation, and he noticed some things that may not have been pointed out before. Chief among them was the fact that the Greek used in Revelation was relatively crude and sometimes grammatically incorrect, while the Greek used in the Gospel of John and the letters of John was much more sophisticated. Dionysus offered the opinion that someone other than John the Apostle had authored Revelation.

The debate has raged ever since. Over the last few decades, one popular theory is that some portions of Revelation were written by

John the Baptist and the rest by his followers. Many detailed arguments are offered on behalf of other Johns as well. In the final analysis, we do not know with absolute certainty who wrote Revelation. In this book, for the sake of convenience, we will assume with the mainstream of Christian tradition that the author is John the Apostle, and we will often refer to him simply as "John of Patmos."

This much is clear: Revelation was composed by an author steeped in the Old Testament. Of the 404 verses in Revelation, an astounding 278 contain Old Testament references (Metzger, 13). Many of what we regard as the strange images of Revelation are actually reworked images from books like Isaiah, Zechariah, and Daniel. Our inadequate knowledge of the Old Testament, especially the prophets, is likely one reason that we struggle so much with Revelation.

As for when the Apocalypse was written, most scholars now believe it was near the end of the reign of the Roman emperor Domitian in about AD 95. Domitian's reign ended in the year 96. A few decades before Domitian, something dramatic occurred in Rome. The practice of emperor worship took hold. The Roman Senate elected Caesar as god, actually voting to deify him. Subsequently, Rome erected altars to Caesar across the empire and established an imperial priesthood to promote his worship. This was primarily a political move designed to ensure loyalty from disparate nations and peoples in a sometimes unwieldy empire. Not all the emperors took it seriously.

Domitian, however, took it extremely seriously. Perhaps this arose from his insecurity. He was an unstable personality and was highly disliked by many Roman leaders (*Interpreter's Bible*, 12:355). Claiming to be God, if you can pull it off, is a good defense against your enemies. In fact, Caesar claimed that all the people in his family were gods and that he himself was a direct descendant of the gods. As such, he commanded public sacrifices in his honor and insisted in his household that he be called "our Lord and our God."

Historically, all Jews were exempted from the requirement to worship the emperor, but, by the time of Domitian, Christians were no longer seen as a sect within Judaism but as a separate religion. Therefore, they lost their exemption and were compelled by Roman law to worship Caesar. When they decided to stay true to God and refuse, they threatened Domitian's authority, and he came after them with all the vengeance of an insecure dictator. Many scholars point out that Domitian's persecutions may not have been so bad. They were spotty and not as widespread as some have thought, but they were nevertheless enough to induce terror in the early church. By comparison, terrorist attacks on American soil today have been few, but because of them we line up at security checkpoints in our airports and listen to blaring speakers tell us what color alert the new Department of Homeland Security has declared today. A little persecution goes a long way.

Make no mistake: in spite of Dionysus's observation that Revelation was written in relatively crude Greek, Revelation is a work of art that was crafted in a dangerous time. As such, it was written with layers of meaning that we must peel back one at a time. The first layer of meaning in Revelation is the word it speaks to its immediate historical situation. It still has meaning for the present and the future, but failure to understand its first-century meaning leads to gross misinterpretations of the other layers of Revelation. That is because what John's vision means for our day and what it means for the end times are related to what it meant for the first century.

Revelation gave first-century Christians the strength to endure their suffering. This strength was offered through a promise: when the curtain comes down on history, God will finally prevail. In other words, they could endure because they knew that Caesar's word was not the last word. The end times are described in Revelation as the solution to the present problems of its readers. That is, Revelation is not a playbook for the final days but a promise of deliverance to those who are victimized by evil. John also says that this message is for "all the churches," and so we know that its message is for us, too, as we await the destruction of evil in a fallen world.

What Kind of Writing Is It?

Most of us have never read another book like Revelation, and many of us do not quite know what to make of it. It will be an enormous help if we can understand what kind of writing it is. Actually, Revelation involves several kinds of writing, several of them unfamiliar to us today, all melded into one.

APOCALYPSE

"Apocalypse" is the Greek word for revelation, and the first verse of Revelation uses this word to describe itself. Because of this,

Revelation is often referred to as "the Apocalypse." Other ancient books claimed to reveal the purposes of God in history (Beasley-Murray, 14) and told of beasts, dragons, and other figures that are wondrous and sometimes semi-human. Scholars call such books apocalyptic literature. Most apocalypses are Jewish writings, composed in a period in which Israel was under constant threat from Rome, but some of them are Christian, composed in a similar situation of oppression. Revelation is the only apocalypse included in the New Testament, but apocalyptic style heavily influenced the last half of the book of Daniel. Apocalyptic passages also appear in the prophets and in the "Little Apocalypse," which is included in Matthew, Mark, and Luke. This type of writing was popular from about two centuries before Christ (around the time most scholars believe Daniel was written) until shortly after the fall of Jerusalem and the collapse of the Jewish nation in AD 70.

Apocalypses were attempts to unveil truths that were beyond ordinary human experience, and so they employed images that were beyond ordinary human experience. These images are often highly symbolic and somewhat fluid. Apocalyptic writers were more poets than chroniclers, more dramatists than historians. When understood, the apocalyptic style is not a barrier to understanding Revelation but a means of expressing truth that is inexpressible in normal human language.

Moviemakers and popular authors today are drawn to the word "apocalypse," and they use it frequently to evoke the specter of fear and suffering and doom. This is good for selling movies and books, but we should be wary of thinking of the Apocalypse of John in the same way. Revelation is not just a horror-movie depiction of the end of the world, and it is not just a book full of gratuitous violence. In fact, it is the opposite. Certainly, it is a book is filled with warnings and violent images, but the bottom line of Revelation is hope. Its horrors are most often put forth in describing the destruction of the evil that afflicts us. The joy of this liberation results in Revelation's magnificent doxologies, which have lifted spirits and inspired great works of art for twenty centuries. In case you have missed it, Handel's *Messiah* is right out of the pages of Revelation.

EPISTLE

It surprises many people to learn that the book of Revelation is actually a letter. Some of us know that it contains seven letters to the churches of the province of Asia, but 1:4-6 says that Revelation as a whole is a letter to these churches.

This is important for determining how we understand Revelation. If Revelation is a letter to seven specific churches, then Revelation, like the letters of Paul, addresses a particular historical set of circumstances. We are not free to ignore these circumstances any more than we would be free to ignore the situation in the church at Corinth when Paul wrote to speak to its people's problems. In fact, the letters to the seven churches in chapters 2 and 3 are included in John's Apocalypse precisely so that we will know what those churches were dealing with when we read the rest of the book.

It is also important that Revelation is addressed to churches and not to individuals. This book of hope speaks to what the people of these seven churches are experiencing together. There is no lone ranger religion in Revelation, no being spiritual without a community of faith. Perhaps this is why the early church found Revelation to be worthy of inclusion in the Bible, even though many Christians at the time thought it should have been omitted.

PROPHECY

A third kind of writing that dominates Revelation is prophecy. Scholars like Robert Mounce hold the opinion that Revelation is more prophecy than apocalypse (Mounce, *NIC*, 8). Most of us grow up thinking of prophecy as predictions of the future. A close study of the Hebrew prophets, however, reveals that prophecy is much more than that. Prophecy is a warning call from God. It thunders its judgments of moral and spiritual evils. It tells of the future that awaits an unrepentant people, and it holds out hope to those who turn from their ways. Prophetic predictions always come in this context, and they are always shaped by the events of the time in which they are delivered.

This is the very nature of Revelation. Like prophecy, Revelation declares "God's demand on man now in the light of his acts of judgment and grace" (Beasley-Murray, 20). The Apocalypse of John is more than a word about the future: it is a word for the present. Like prophecy, Revelation warns the people of the judgment of God. Like prophecy, Revelation spotlights the coming Day of the Lord and presents promises that stir our deepest hopes. This promise of hope, this bright optimism, is the bottom line of Revelation. Others might see only doom at the end of history, but John sees "a new heaven and a new earth" (21:1). Others might see the world ending with either a bang or a whimper (as T. S. Eliot said in "The Hollow Men," 1925), but John sees it ending in a city of eternal light where there is no more death and where there are no more tears.

A Prayer for this Book

The book of Revelation has as much to say to our age as any book in the Bible. Unfortunately, however, its voice is now muffled by the ages and twisted by misunderstanding. Sadly, most of us never actually read it. Rather than turning to the book itself, we allow itinerant preachers, popular books, and elaborate charts to shape our understanding. When we do turn to it, its content is so confusing that it might as well be written in Sanskrit as far as most Christians are concerned. So we simply shrug our shoulders and say, "I'll never understand it."

It is important that we gain a good understanding of Revelation. Grievous misinterpretations abound, and they drive more people away from the faith than they draw to it. They obscure the word of God. They cause many Christians to miss the life-giving message of this part of Scripture. They lead to often-dangerous views on current geopolitical issues that were never intended by the author of Revelation or the God who inspired it.

The purpose of this Sessions Series study is to help the reader recover Revelation and hear its real message, perhaps for the first time. This is not possible without the hard work of slogging through difficult passages and thinking through tough issues. Neither is it possible without "un-teaching" ourselves a great deal of what we have already learned, but treasures await those who persevere.

The message of Revelation, after all, is a "must hear." It really is a revelation from God. My prayer is that this study will take you on a journey through Revelation that will open your mind, quicken your heart, stimulate your hope, and enlarge your vision of God. My prayer is that you will allow the poetry and drama of Revelation to help you "come up here" (4:1 and 11:12) into the knowledge of God. If you take it seriously, at the end of this study you may find that the same book that has always struck fear in your soul now strikes hope instead. The Apocalypse of John has the power to change your life.

It All Begins with Worship

Revelation 1:1-20

It's a strange thing about God: God comes nearest when we worship. I suppose this is why one of the biblical writers said, "Draw near to God, and he will draw near to you" (Jas 4:8a). The Bible is full of stories of the presence of God, most of them occurring when people worship. Moses, for example, stood on holy ground before the burning bush and took off his shoes, and when he did, he met God. Isaiah went to the temple to worship. While he was there, God came, and "the hem of his robe filled the temple" (Isa 6:1b). A little crowd in Nazareth went to the synagogue to worship, and their hometown boy, Jesus, read from Isaiah, implying to them that he himself was God's Messiah (Luke 4:16-30). Paul saw a light and literally fell to the ground. Before him was the very Jesus whom he was persecuting (Acts 9:3-5).

God does sometimes surprise us with his presence, but we could make a strong argument that he most often reveals himself when we stand awestruck before him. This is where the book of Revelation begins. Before John could hear God's call to "come up hither" (4:1), John had to be attuned to the voice of God. Then, when he came into the presence of God, he was prepared for what he was about to see. Before looking at the story of that experience, however, we need to examine the important words of introduction in the first few verses of Revelation.

John's Introduction to Revelation (1:1-8)

Revelation takes its name from the first phrase of the book: "The revelation of Jesus Christ." John spells out the nature of his writing up front. Revelation is a revealing of the promises and purposes of God, and this revelation is from Jesus Christ himself. In other words, John says that Revelation is not just his own imagination in overdrive. It is a word directly from God.

The things that are to be revealed, John says, will "soon" take place (v. 1). Perhaps this is an allusion to the early Christians' belief that Christ would return in their lifetimes, but it is more likely that the word "soon" is used here in God's context of time. The message to suffering first-century believers is that their trials are not forever. God will "soon" make an end of them. Whatever "soon" may mean, the book of Revelation ends with a reaffirmation of Jesus' promise to come soon. Obviously, the use of the word was not accidental.

John says that the revelation was given to him to be shared with others, so it is safe to presume that it was meant to be understood. Many people do not find Revelation understandable. In the first century, however, readers had encountered other documents written in the strange apocalyptic style of Revelation, and so it would have been less obscure to them than it is to us. They were also more familiar with its many Old Testament references than we are, which would have helped them to understand this book more easily than we do. Revelation was not, by the way, written in code to prevent outsiders from understanding it. While many have propounded this theory, the Romans would have had no trouble figuring out that the book was speaking of them when it referred to Satan's instrument on earth. As strange as it may sound to modern ears, Revelation was intended to be understood.

Still, we often have a great deal of trouble unlocking the message of Revelation. Misunderstandings abound and are widely believed. Countless commentators read ideas into Revelation that are not there. For instance, the rapture is never mentioned in Revelation, nor is the word "antichrist" used a single time. Some have interpreted the "Come up hither" of Revelation 4:1 as an invitation to John to come up to heaven as a part of the rapture, when all believers, dead and alive, meet Christ in the air and are taken by him into heaven, but this is not what the verse says. There is no mention of rapture, resurrection from the dead, or masses of believers floating upward. Revelation 4:1 is just what it says it is: an invitation to John to enter the courts of heaven and receive a revelation to be delivered to the seven churches. There seems to be one way to find the rapture in this verse: by reading a possible vision of the rapture from 1 Thessalonians into the text in a place where it makes no sense. This is a dubious way to read the Bible. Any interpretation of Scripture that is not evident within the text itself is suspect. Scripture means what it says, not what someone imagines it says.

John clearly did not want his readers to give up on Revelation because it is difficult. Yet I have heard pastors say that they do not preach on Revelation because they do not understand it. John's great but mysterious book has an essential and powerful message for the Christian community. We should not ignore it. Even if we must work hard to understand it, the message delivered by John of Patmos is not one we should miss.

One reason Revelation is difficult for us to understand is that the centuries have obscured what God did not. Revelation was written largely as an apocalypse, a literary type that achieved some popularity in the first century but that has long since disappeared. Our consequent lack of familiarity with any apocalyptic writing other than Revelation makes the imagery and nature of the book strange to us. Also, since most of us are not familiar with the historical circumstances addressed by Revelation, not all of its references make immediate sense to us. In fact, many deny that Revelation addresses any historical circumstance (in spite of the fact that John says in 1:4 that it does) except our own. This viewpoint results in strange understandings of the book that must be revised each time another generation passes without the return of Christ. Unfortunately, these misunderstandings have dominated popular discourse about the book.

Of course, Revelation is not intended only for first-century Christians. The number of the churches is seven, a number that represents completeness and implies that, at a second level, this is a message to all Christ's churches of all the ages. Still, before we can understand what the Apocalypse is saying to us, we must understand what it was saying in the time in which it was written.

As John wrote, the churches of Asia Minor were under stress, and this trouble was probably the reason for John's exile on Patmos. The Roman emperor at the time was Domitian, and he was obsessed with maintaining his own power in the face of opposition. One of the ways he did this was by enforcing the idea and practice of emperor worship. Early Christianity had spread rapidly in Asia Minor, and Christians there refused to acknowledge his claims to divinity. Domitian saw this resistance as a political threat, and he responded by persecuting Christians. Believers were often harassed and sometimes martyred. Their fear had become so great that some had fallen away from the church. In the face of this persecution,

Christians were largely powerless. The book of Revelation was written precisely to speak to their need. It brought a word from God to them that said, in effect, "My power is greater is greater than that of your oppressors and greater than that of Satan. Do not be afraid of their attacks. I will deliver you."

John opens the Apocalypse with the same greeting that is common in Paul's letters: "Grace to you and peace" (1:4). These words have never been more significant than they are here. The seven churches had received anything but grace and peace from their persecutors, but now grace and peace are extended to them in the form of a revelation from God.

John mentions three sources for this grace and peace. First, it comes "from him who is and who was and who is to come" (v. 4). This is a beautiful way of describing the God who lives beyond time, and it is used on several occasions in Revelation. Second, this grace and peace come from the "seven spirits which are before the throne" (1:4). The seven spirits, mentioned three more times in Revelation (in 3:1, 4:5, and 5:6), could represent the Holy Spirit, or, more likely, they could represent heavenly beings. Third, this grace and peace come from Jesus Christ who is the faithful witness, the firstborn of the dead, and the ruler of kings on earth. This final phrase about kings sounds a note that we have already heard: God is more powerful than Caesar; those who follow him need not fear him.

This introduction to the Apocalypse ends with two strong affirmations, each expressed in soaring and beautiful prose. Verse 7 reads, "Behold, he is coming with the clouds, and every eye will see him, every one who pierced him; and all tribes of the earth will wail on account of him. Even so. Amen." John's language here was probably inspired by Daniel 7:13, which says, "Behold, one like the Son of man came with the clouds of heaven." These clouds have often been depicted as literal, but John probably did not intend this. If he had, we would be hard pressed to explain how every eye could see him at once. It would be impossible for him to appear physically on every side of a round earth at the same time. If, however, the clouds are evocative images intended to say that he will return from a beyond that is as yet unknown to us, then the passage no longer poses geographical problems. Christ returning on the clouds becomes a mental picture of a spiritual phenomenon. He will return and will spiritually appear to the whole of creation at once.

We need not concern ourselves with the physical manifestation of this teaching.

A second affirmation (1:8) helps to draw John's introduction to a close. God declares, "I am the Alpha and the Omega." These are the first and last letters of the Greek alphabet, and they remind us that God was our beginning and will be our end, that he was our origin and will be our destiny. He is the one, we are reminded again, "who was and is and is to come."

John's Encounter with God (1:9-20)

From Revelation 1:9 to the end of the chapter, John describes the worship experience that was his initial encounter with God. He starts by identifying with the seven churches to whom his account is addressed. He assures them that he shares with them not only their tribulations but also the kingdom of God itself. He also shares the pain of being rejected for his faith and the blessing of finding strength to endure.

He tells them how God came to him even on Patmos, an island that some believed was God-forsaken. Like the psalmist in Psalm 139, John discovers that no place is bereft of the presence of God (Ps 139:7). John is "in the Spirit on the Lord's day" when he hears a loud voice behind him. Even though he is alone in exile, he is keeping track of time; he knows when the Sabbath is. This enables him to be ready to enter the presence of God when the holy day arrives.

Real worship is always a meeting with mystery, an encounter with that which is beyond our understanding. Real worship overwhelms, engulfs, and renders speechless all those who behold the beauty of God. John's worship humbles his spirit. His personal agenda fades so that the glory of God can consume the moment.

Revelation always begins with such an experience. Before the agenda of God can become the center of our focus, the voice of God must drown out our personal agendas. Only when this happens can we hear a new word from the Eternal. So it is that a loud voice speaks to John, a voice like a trumpet, clear and strong and beautiful, and it charges him to write down what he is about to see and then share it with the seven churches. To this voice, John can only surrender.

When John turns (v. 12) to see where the voice is coming from, he beholds "one like a son of man." Daniel 7:13 used this term to denote the Messiah, and other Jewish writings before the birth of

Christ also used it in this way. John makes clear that the figure at the heart of his revelation is Jesus Christ himself. Since this one like a son of man will give John the letters to deliver to the seven churches, I will from here forward refer to the author of the seven letters as the Christ. As we will see, the book of Revelation often minimizes the distinction between Christ and God.

Christ is standing in the midst of seven golden lampstands. Those lampstands symbolize the seven churches (v. 20). Like lampstands, the churches give light in a shadowy world. They are said to be golden, even though they are flawed. Flawed congregations, flawed leaders, flawed theology, and flawed practice do not erode their value. They are golden lampstands. They are the churches of God.

Christ wears a long robe and a sash, the traditional garments of the high priest. He is like a high priest. He makes intercession for suffering believers and brings comfort to the people of God. He leads the lesser priests who serve him. John also says he has hair that is "white like wool" (just like "the Ancient of Days" in Dan 7:9), indicating that he has the wisdom and maturity of the ages.

His eyes are "like blazing fire," able to see into the hidden places of the soul, into the darkness in which we so often hide our guilt. His feet are like bronze, strong and sure beneath him. His voice is like the many waters, powerful and pure, life giving and cleansing.

In his right hand, he holds seven stars, one for each of the angels of the seven churches. The word "angel" means messenger, and it is noteworthy that each church is said to have an angel. This means that every church has a messenger from God, one who encourages and corrects, stands by and protects, and emboldens them in the face of the hostility of the world.

The message for the churches of all times is that there is always a message from God and always an angel trying to deliver it. Sometimes the message is one of judgment, for our churches are not perfect. Sometimes the message is one of encouragement, for every church has times when discouragement nearly takes over. Sometimes the message is one of hope, for so many have given up on the future. Sometimes the message is one of mission, because it is so easy for churches to be captured by the past and miss opportunities to carry out their missions today. I know one church whose community has changed from rural to small town to suburban to international in a little over a century. The church has adapted to every change. I know another church that has a passion for ministering to the homeless, and another that has helped to end certain diseases in third-world nations. I know another church that has bound up the wounds of a whole community in the name of Christ for two hundred years, and still another that has honed its evangelistic witness with effectiveness and integrity. There are all kinds of possible explanations for how these churches have accomplished what they have, but I think John would have said that they listened to their angels.

A two-edged sword proceeds from the mouth of Jesus in John's vision. This sword is the Word of God. In the beginning, God used the Word to create. In the present, he uses the Word to redeem. In the end, he will use the Word to conquer. This double-edged sword cuts in any direction that it is wielded. It will destroy the forces of darkness that are arrayed against the churches.

This magnificent opening scene of Revelation ends with one crowning detail: Christ's face shone like the noonday sun. Nothing in all creation could outshine his glory, his hope, his joy. This description shows the glory of the presence of God and the majesty of God's surroundings. It paints a picture of a court more magnificent than Caesar's, where God reigns with power greater than any other. Nothing more should be read into it. John's words are artfully and powerfully inspired, and we should hear them for what they are.

John's reaction to this incomprehensible scene is to fall prone and still before God, over-awed by the presence. This is the highest expression of worship—to fall down "as though dead" before God, to stand with mouth open at the beauty of his presence, to wait with tongue stilled, stunned into silence by a Word so pure that no human tongue can even stammer in its presence. To truly worship is to be overcome and overtaken by God.

Christ puts his right hand on the fallen John and tells him not to fear. Christ is, after all, the eternal one, the one with the keys to Death and Hades. John of Patmos has no reason to be afraid.

"Now write what you have seen" (1:19a), says the Christ with the keys, and John writes exactly that. He has seen the glory. He has experienced the presence. He has fallen before something greater than himself. Now John is ready to see what is to come. It began with worship. It always does.

1. Discuss the circumstances under which Revelation was written. Why were the Christians in this region being persecuted? Who was persecuting them?

_____

_____

_____

_____

_____

2. To whom is Revelation addressed, and what was the purpose for writing it?

_____

_____

_____

_____

_____

3. Describe the scene John witnessed when he responded to the loud voice on the Lord's Day. What did the seven stars and the seven lampstands represent?

_____

_____

_____

_____

_____

4. What has Revelation 1 taught you about worship?

_____

_____

_____

_____

_____

5. What is your mental picture of the return of Christ?

_____

_____

_____

_____

_____

The Letters to the Seven Churches

Revelation 2–3

Pop culture often views churches as either boringly irrelevant or hypocritically corrupt. The New Testament views them quite differently, seeing them as footholds of the kingdom of God on earth. This high New Testament view of the church is seen clearly in the fact that much of the New Testament, including practically all the writings of Paul, are written not to individual believers but to churches.

This profound concern for churches (not only for the church universal but also for individual local congregations) is reflected in the book of Revelation. Revelation as a whole is a letter to seven churches to give them hope amid trying circumstances. Within the larger letter are seven individual letters addressing the particular circumstances of each congregation.

These letters are contained in chapters 2 and 3. They are perhaps the most easily understandable section of Revelation because the churches they address are much like the ones we know. The failures and successes of these churches are like the failures and successes of our churches, and the problems and victories of these churches are like the problems and victories of ours.

Each letter offers a spiritual diagnosis of the congregation to which it is addressed. Today we often diagnose churches sociologically. We assess factors like the social conditions of the communities in which the churches minister, the stages of their congregational development, the styles of their lay and clergy leadership, and the internal dynamics that affect their institutional health. The letters in Revelation, however, do not offer sociological analyses of the churches. They offer spiritual diagnoses, a type of diagnosis that church strategists of our time are often reluctant to give. While social circumstances strongly affect churches, what matters most in Revelation is not how the churches have responded to their communities but how they have responded to God.

The letters appear immediately after the book of Revelation is introduced, and they provide a kind of preface for the rest of the book. In each of the letters, Christ says in essence, "I know you. I know what great things you have done and what courage you have shown. I know where you struggle and I know where you fail. I know how easy it would be for you to surrender to your enemies. You have shown me how frightened and weak you are, and I have called you to a higher standard; now let me show you a vision of glory that will help you persevere."

Persecution of the early church did not come from only one source. The churches faced persecution from the local authorities, the Roman government, the synagogues in their communities, and neighbors who were fearful of what they were up to. If the Christian movement was to survive, the churches had to be strong. This is why the book of Revelation was written. It is neither a book obsessed with end-time details nor a book intended to frighten people into conversion with tales of beasts and dragons; it is a book that calls churches, often troubled ones, to hope, to oppose evil, and to share with the world the unbelievable promises of God. These letters affirmed and corrected each of the churches in order to prepare them for what was about to be unveiled and to strengthen them for the mission to which they were called. They would need it. More hardship duty lay ahead.

Despite their uniqueness, the seven letters share some features with each other. All are letters from the one "who holds the seven stars in his right hand, who walks among the seven golden lampstands" (2:1). (Revelation 1:12-16 makes it clear that this one is Christ, or God. Since the Apocalypse minimizes the distinction between God and Jesus the Christ, and since the one who walks among the lampstands is said to be "one like a son of man," I will refer to the sender of the letters as the Christ.) Each letter begins with Christ instructing the angel of that church to write. Each contains an opening phrase indicating that he knows them. Most often the phrase is, "I know your works." Each letter gives a critique of the individual church, including a positive appraisal in the case of all the churches and a negative one in the case of five of them. Finally, each letter concludes with an admonition: "Let anyone who has an ear listen to what the Spirit is saying to the churches."

The Church that Lost Its Love: Ephesus (2:1-7)

Ephesus was one of the great cities of the ancient world. The church there had a strong influence that it had used well for the cause of Christ. Its members had patiently endured hostility. They had refused to tolerate evildoers. They had rejected the Nicolaitans (a short-lived sect that apparently believed no restraints should be placed on the behavior of Christians). They had identified and weeded out false apostles. The first of the letters to the churches does not hold back praise for these achievements.

Perhaps pride was a temptation for the church at Ephesus. They served in the second city of the Roman Empire in the shadow of one of the Seven Wonders of the Ancient World, the famous Temple of Artemis. The founder of their church was Paul, and he had made his headquarters with them for three years (Acts 20:31). The great apostle had written their church a beautiful and thoughtful letter that they had carefully preserved. Finally, if the legend is correct, both the apostle John and Mary the mother of Jesus lived out their last years in Ephesus and would almost certainly have been a part of this church.

If the Ephesian church had become a bit too proud of all this, it would have been no surprise. Neither would it have been a surprise that their pride led them to a fall (see Proverbs 16). They letter to them from Christ pulled no punches about their failures: The church had abandoned the love it had when it was founded. The people's ardor for God had cooled, and they had grown weary of doing well. Predictably, their works diminished along with their love. Christ's letter speaks harshly: if you do not change, your lampstand will be removed. With no deep love for God, they will be left with no light to share.

When churches become too proud, when they do no more than erect grand edifices on street corners and admire themselves, when the monuments they build are in their own honor and not God's, when they revel in the esteem of their community or their leadership in the community of churches, then their members are acting no differently than the people of this world. When on the other hand they serve the weak, give their presence to the dying, share their strength with the lame, lend their sight to the blind and their ears to the deaf, when they put the broken together again, visit the lonely, soothe the fearful, and point those who have lost their way to the Way that leads to life, then they are acting as the people of God. This is the lesson of Ephesus.

The Church that Endured: Smyrna (2:8-11)

The church at Smyrna was persecuted with special intensity. Whenever the church's leaders gathered, no doubt they were frightened and anxious people. At times, some members of their group were afraid to come to worship. Surely they suspected that some of them would soon be martyred. They had no means of resistance, no unbiased court in which to plead their case, no influential people who were on their side, and no friendly officials who would give them grace. With no earthly hope of deliverance from this onslaught of opposition, they wilted quickly. Some abandoned the church and renounced the faith, and the pressure to do this mounted with every successive wave of hostility.

The Smyrnean church was under extreme duress. Perhaps that is the reason it received no rebuke from the Christ, but only encouragement and compassion. "I know your affliction . . ." (2:9), said God, and those words must have fallen on them like rain on desert sands. They had been made weak, but the presence of the Strong One was the most comforting grace they could have received. His presence may not have removed their suffering, but it gave them the strength to endure.

The letter to Smyrna held out to that battered church two reasons to hope. One was the offer of a crown of life. The other was the assurance that their suffering would be short. "Be faithful unto death," says the Living One, "and I will give you the crown of life" (2:10b). Life here is presented as a precious gift and is promised, ironically, to those who die in faith. Who else could bestow a crown of life upon the dead but one who had power over death itself? To the believers at Smyrna, the Spirit was saying, "Even if you are killed for my sake, I will still give you the splendor and the grace of life."

The second ray of hope was offered to those "the devil is about to throw . . . into prison" (2:10). Their affliction will last for only ten days. This is not a literal ten days, but a symbolic ten days indicating a short period. This promise said to the Christians at Smyrna, "You have suffered, and even when greater suffering comes upon you, it will not last forever. I will call an end."

Interestingly, a historical event suggests that this letter did strengthen Smyrnean believers as they faced persecution. A young

Christian named Polycarp apparently lived in Smyrna at this time. His story is remarkable.

When Polycarp grew much older, he became the bishop in Smyrna and one of the most brilliant leaders of the early church. He had almost certainly been aware of this letter to his church from his early youth. He faced his own cross in about AD 155 when the Romans condemned him to die. The Roman proconsul, or governor, offered Polycarp the opportunity to save himself by renouncing Christ and swearing allegiance to Caesar, but Polycarp declined: "Eighty and six years I have served him, and he never did me any injury. How then can I blaspheme my King and Savior?" (*Martyrdom of Polycarp* 9).

Then the Proconsul said, "I will cause you to be consumed by fire, seeing you despise the wild beasts, if you will not repent."

Polycarp replied, "You threaten me with fire which burns for an hour, and after a little is extinguished, but are ignorant of the fire of the coming judgment and of eternal punishment, reserved for the ungodly. But why do you tarry? Bring forth what you will" (*Martyrdom of Polycarp* 11). Then the great saint was tied to a stake and a fire was kindled at his feet. According to legend, the flames did not consume him, and so they stabbed him to death. Perhaps he found the power to speak with such courage in some words from the old letter to his church: "Be faithful until death, and I will give you the crown of life" (2:10b).

The Church at Satan's Throne: Pergamum (2:12-17)

Pergamum was the capital city of the province of Asia, which lay in the western-most part of Asia Minor and was home to all of the seven churches. The church in Pergamum had its issues, perhaps partly related to the fact that it was a religious center. A statue of Zeus dominated the city from its perch on an 800-foot hill. The first temple to Augustus built in Asia Minor was located there. As the capital city, it was the official seat of emperor worship in that region, and so it earned the designation, "Satan's throne" (2:13).

The heart of the letter to Pergamum was an accusation that the church harbored factions that followed false teachings. One group followed the Nicolaitans, that obscure and lawless group we met at Ephesus. Another followed the Baalamites, a group named for Baalam, a kind of prophet-for-hire whose story is told in Numbers 22. The Baalamites ate meat sacrificed to idols and, through this action, led people to worship false gods. (Most likely, the word "fornication" as it appears here refers to this spiritual unfaithfulness rather than sexual sin. This would be consistent with the way John uses similar terms in the rest of the Apocalypse.)

The fact that the letter refers to Pergamum as Satan's throne, then, is not surprising, but it is a particularly harsh reference that almost certainly offended the citizens of Pergamum. Still, Christ held nothing back in speaking to them in words that were, as someone once said, stronger than eight acres of garlic. This city was rife with emperor worship and sectarian belief. This church at Pergamum had tried to cope by blending the heresies around it with the Christian faith. Christ's judgment on their behavior was harsh.

This problem, often called syncretism, has persisted throughout the history of the church. Believers are always bending their knees to new Caesars and building new thrones for Satan. Yet the church usually speaks to them tenderly, fearing that if their words are too harsh, the compromisers will reject the faith altogether. Christ's words to the church at Pergamum remind us that words of faith must sometimes be confrontational. When believers allow other human beings to starve, the church cannot speak mildly. When our culture yields its young people to the curse of drug addiction and prefers punishment over treatment, the church cannot speak mildly. When governments condone torture, no matter the purpose, the church cannot speak mildly. When Christians themselves give no advantage to the weak, have no compassion for the poor, rob God in their tithes and offerings, and neglect justice for the sake of financial gain, the church cannot speak mildly. Revelation is not only apocalypse; it is also prophecy. Like the books of prophecy that have come before, it lends a reverberant voice to the righteous anger of God.

The letter calls the Pergamum church to banish the worship of false gods. If the church fails to heed this call, Christ is quite clear about the consequences: the Lord will simply show up in Pergamum and make war against those who have betrayed him (2:16). "Christ will make war on them?" we ask. "That sounds pretty harsh, don't you think? Will he bomb the church? Will he bring in the drones." No. The Scripture says he will make war with the sharp sword that is in his mouth. That sword is the word of God. If the church does not heed his word, he will hold truth painfully before it so that its congregation will abandon their ways. God never makes war with a dull sword. His word cuts to the heart of the matter. The church must repent.

Now, the tone shifts. The voice of the Christ grows warm as he extends his promises to those who are faithful. He promises them manna from heaven and a white stone. Manna is a symbol familiar to us. It means that he will feed their strength so that they might endure all that will befall them. This is exactly what he did when he gave manna to Israel as it followed Moses into the wilderness. The white stone is less familiar to us. It was a symbol of protection, probably inspired by the first-century popularity of amulets, stones that afforded their bearers protection from trouble. The white stone meant that Christ would give faithful protection from the assault of Satan. On this stone a new name would be written, the name of the risen Christ, the only one who is able to offer real protection. The name on the stone, the letter says, can be known, or understood, only by those who receive it. Those who receive the stone understand what Christ's name means. To those who have not received the stone, it is an incomprehensible mystery.

The Church that Went Along: Thyatira (2:18-29)

The church at Thyatira was so flexible it could have fit in anywhere. If some of its members wished to follow the Nicolaitans and dispense with the onerous requirements of morality, that was fine. If others wanted to listen to the Baalamites and blend other faiths with Christianity, that was fine too. They were open to a fault, and this characteristic got them in trouble with Christ. He sent them a letter, and in it he made it clear that their practices were unacceptable.

Particularly problematic was the situation with the trade guilds. In order to work in Thyatira, a person had to be a member of a trade guild. The guilds had a religious dimension, however, and at their meetings they ate a common meal at which they consumed meat that had been sacrificed to idols in an act of religious devotion. For many Christians there, participation in this meal amounted to a betrayal of their faith. A woman in Thyatira called Jezebel encouraged the believers to go along, to pretend they were something they were not for the sake of economic gain. Perhaps she was called Jezebel because she was so much like Jezebel of the Old Testament, who actually set up an altar to Baal in the temple in Jerusalem. Christ called the unfaithful followers of the Thyatiran Jezebel to repentance.

The temptation to blend the faith remains an issue for churches. That is particularly true in a day when we are learning more about other religions than ever before. Also, in my view, a primary example of syncretism is the desire expressed by many people today to be "spiritual but not religious."

This trend appeared at first (to me at least) to be an effort to get back to a basic and honest spirituality. It was born in part in reaction to the self-serving spirit and the corruption that often mark "organized religion." Then, however, the spirituality took on many of the markings of the culture. This is usually a highly individualistic kind of spirituality, taking its cues form a highly individualistic culture. The fatal flaw of this trend is that it exalts the individual and devalues the group. This approach has not proven to be workable in human history. "Spiritual but not religious" spirituality usually adopts an anti-institutional character, basking in its hostility not only to corrupted forms of organized religion but to all forms of organized religion. This anti-institutionalism, of course, is one of the strongest marks of contemporary culture.

I view this kind of spirituality as guilty of the sin of syncretism because it mixes a cultural faith with the Christian faith, and the result is something less than Christian. The God whom Christians worship is above culture. The God whom Christians worships actually seems to care about institutions, for instance, the nation Israel and the Christian church. Mixing pop-spirituality-of-the-culture faith with biblical faith is not substantially different from the early believers in Thyatira blending the guild-god of their culture with the eternal God who was in Christ.

The believers at Thyatira, of course, were not totally corrupt. Christ was quick to commend their redeeming qualities. He honored their love, their faith, their service, and their patient endurance, all larger-than-life virtues and all deserving much greater reflection than we can give them here. The church at Thyatira had what it needed to hold fast. If they succeeded, then Christ promised that they would one day be conquerors and rule with him over the nations (2:26). Until that day, they would have "the morning star" (2:28), the light of Christ's Spirit, to guide them.

The Church that Was Already Dead: Sardis (3:1-6)

The letter to the church at Sardis came right to the point: the church was dead. It had a reputation for being alive, but it was not. If it had any life at all, it was a false life. It could have had the best children's program in town, the best preaching, the best choir, the best praise team, the best social media strategy, and the friendliest members. Some of the members of other churches in the area could well have said to their pastors, "Let's be like Sardis! They're packing 'em in. They're doing something right!" Christ, however, knew that all was not well. Beneath the vitality that appeared on the surface of that congregation was a lifeless core.

Perhaps there were good reasons for the Sardis church to be in this condition. Their circumstances were relatively easy. There was no significant Jewish-Christian tension in their city, since few Jews lived there. There was a relatively low level of tension between Christians and the authorities, probably due to the fact that Sardis was not a center of emperor worship. Perhaps these circumstances allowed them to experience little persecution, but the same circumstances probably also made the church vulnerable to apathy. Certainly we know that in relaxed situations, churches have always had a tendency to become so comfortable, so accepted, so established that their life force begins to ebb. On the other hand, when churches have suffered persecution, they have often thrived. This is true in many places today. It was so true in the early church that Tertullian, one of the great leaders of the second-century church, said in a now famous phrase, "The blood of the martyrs is the seed of the church" (*Apologeticus* 50). Perhaps the opposite is true as well: the life of the comfortable may signal the death of their churches.

The description of Sardis applies easily to many churches in the Western world today. For example, they seem to wither in the soft circumstances of North America and Europe, but they thrive in more difficult places like Africa and Asia. To churches like Sardis that have mistaken spiritual death for spiritual life, Christ issues a call to wake up to his presence. "If you are not awake to my presence," he says in effect, "you will not even know when I come to you. Some of you will look about and say that my Spirit is absent from your church and from your life, not knowing that I have already come to you, but you were asleep."

The hope of Sardis was that some of its people would see Christ's presence. A few who were there had not "soiled their clothes" (2:4). They were a remnant, like the one that returned to Israel after the exile. They were the hope of Sardis, and they are the hope of every dead or dying church. The remnant calls the church to life. If the church responds, the believers in that place will find themselves conquerors at the last day. This is the promise of Christ: "If you conquer, you will be clothed like them in white robes, and I will not blot your name out of the book of life . . ." (3:4). Such is the lesson of Sardis.

The Church of the Open Door: Philadelphia (3:7-13)

Perhaps the most compelling image in all of the seven letters is the open door set before the church at Philadelphia. Not a few preachers have found this image helpful in challenging their churches to walk through their own open doors.

It might therefore surprise some of those who have been inspired by these sermons to know that Bible scholars have long debated exactly what was meant by this image of the open door. Most often, it has been understood as an open door of mission and evangelism, and there is a good case to be made for this interpretation. There was a nearly unlimited opportunity for evangelism for the Philadelphian church, and they had every reason to seize it.

Another interpretation is possible, however, and the evidence for it is strong. In the verse prior to the open door reference, Revelation says, "These are the words of the holy one, the true one, who has the key of David, who opens and no one will shut, who shuts and no one opens . . ." (3:7). This verse contrasts with what had happened in Philadelphia. The synagogue there had closed its doors to anyone who followed the Christian way. Now, John draws on Isaiah 22 to say that even though the door to the synagogue is closed, God has opened the door to the kingdom of God. No one except God, no synagogue and no government, can close that door. By this interpretation, the open door is the door to the kingdom of God.

Most interpreters have viewed these two perspectives as mutually exclusive. I have come to believe, however, that both interpretations are valid. An open door to mission does stand before the Philadelphia church, but an open door to the heart and kingdom of God stands before them as well, a door opened by the redeeming act of God in Christ. Having the mind of a poet, John of Patmos is well accustomed to dealing in multiple meanings. It is not unreasonable to think that he has done this here.

The remaining material in the letter is a message of encouragement to a church under fire. The church at Philadelphia faced fearsome opposition. This letter reminded them that some of the opposition was from those "of the synagogue of Satan who say that they are Jews and are not . . ." (3:9a). The Christians of Philadelphia were beaten down and rejected. They had little power to stand in the face of such persecution (3:8), but the message of this letter must have thundered in their ears: "Hold on! I am coming soon, and when I do I will humble your enemies, and then they will know that I have loved you" (3:9b, paraphrased).

In verse 10, Christ praises their "patient endurance" and assures them that he will keep them from "the hour of trial that is coming on the whole world . . . ." John understands that the hour of trial is coming, that evil will intensify as the end approaches. This intensification of evil is referred to in Revelation 7:14 as "the great tribulation." Jesus spoke of this tribulation himself in his Olivet discourse in Matthew's Gospel (Matt 24:9). Some believe that Christ's promise to keep them from the hour of trial means that God will spare the church from the sufferings of the great tribulation at the end of time. This interpretation does not fit well with the rest of the letter to Philadelphia. That is, the remainder of the letter refers to the tribulation in the present. It seems most likely, then, that this is a promise that Christ will sustain them in their present tribulation as they face persecution. As I have studied, I have come to believe that this is a promise that God will protect the church from all tribulations, present and future, and that he will give the church strength to endure until he drops the curtain on human history. Christ promised the believers at Smyrna a crown of life if they endured to the end (2:10). The promise given here means that the same crown awaits the faithful of Philadelphia.

As the letter comes to a close, Christ gives the Philadelphians a final triumphant promise as he repeats, "I am coming soon" (v. 11). This same promise will occur again at the end of Revelation in chapter 22. To Philadelphia, the promise must have seemed like sunshine in a darkened forest. When we read this promise, our first question is often what he meant by "soon." We can be fairly certain that this was not the first question the Philadelphians asked. They were more concerned about hope than about timetables. They were not so much looking for an exact description of the action of God as for the hope of being set free from their present suffering. In these words, they heard the promise, the message of hope. They heard Christ say that he would come to them soon, and they knew that when he came, it would be soon enough.

The Church of the Fading Passion: Laodicea (3:14-22)

Perhaps the most famous of the seven churches is Laodicea, but its fame is not really a positive thing. Laodicea is known for its lack of spiritual passion. Christ accuses the Laodiceans of being "lukewarm" (3:16), and says he will spit the church out of his mouth.

The church at Laodicea was not frozen, but it was nauseatingly tepid.

Spiritual indifference was an enormous problem for Laodicean Christians. They were not hot, and they were not cold, and so God was ready to spit them out of his mouth (3:16). The Greek word, actually much stronger than spit, has often been translated "vomit." Preachers tend to love this translation, because Laodicea seems so much like the churches they serve. The image of God vomiting up the church gives prophetic bite to their congregational castigations.

Lukewarm is of course not acceptable to God. Faith is not meant to be put on "low heat" but to burn white hot. The message to Laodicea is that a church whose heart does not burn hot with the love of God will never be able to warm the cold hearts around it.

Laodicea had another problem as well, one that probably contributed substantially to their lukewarm condition. This was its wealth. Located in a wealthy region of Asia Minor, Laodicea was home to a medical school and a pharmaceutical industry. Ointments for the ears and the eyes were produced in the city and had brought prosperity. In fact, Laodicea's wealth was so great that when it was struck by a catastrophic earthquake in AD 61, it needed no help from Rome in order to rebuild. The Christians there most likely participated in this affluence, especially since they show the signs of spiritual apathy that Jesus so often associated with the wealthy.

Laodicean wealth was probably at the heart of the Laodicean problem. It seems to have made them self-sufficient and proud, as wealth often does. Laodiceans seem to have been scrapping for wealth as though it were the key to heaven itself, but the Jesus the Christians followed had said that it was easier for a camel to pass through the eye of a needle than for the rich to enter the kingdom of God (Matt 19:24). Jesus had also said that no one could serve God and money (Matt 6:24). The Laodiceans seem to have been trying to prove that they were exceptions to the rule.

The truth of Jesus' teachings about the spiritually anesthetizing power of wealth continues to be evident in the world today. Churches in the poorer nations are thriving. Churches in Europe and the United States are largely lethargic, tepid, and shrinking.

The reason for this reality is simple. Wealth is, as Jesus pointed out, spiritually anesthetizing. If that sounds strange to your affluent ears, remember that Jesus repeated teachings to this effect over and over again in the Gospels. Not only did he say that it was easier for a camel to pass through the eye of a needle than for a rich man to enter the kingdom of God (Mark 10:25; Matt 19:24) or that you cannot serve God and money (Matt 6:24); he also said that we should not store up for ourselves treasures on earth (Matt 6:19). He told the rich young man that if he would find eternal life, he must sell all that he had, give the money to the poor, and follow him (Matt 19:21). The most likely reason the Laodicean church grew cool to things of the spirit was that it had become so warmed to things of the flesh. As a result, the church was "wretched, pitiable, poor, blind, naked" (3:17).

Saddest of all, the Laodiceans were not even aware of their state. "You do not realize that you are wretched, pitiable, poor, blind, naked" (3:17), Christ told them. Like so many of the affluent of every place and time, they lived in self-delusion. When the great god mammon (money) commands the hearts of the people of God, what other result would you expect?

Laodicea was the most pitiable of the churches. The message God sent them was plain: You are not what you think you are. Your passion is for something other than God. Therefore, God's judgment is upon you. You must repent and change your ways if you are to have any hope of finding the kingdom.

Prophecy entails more than judgment, however, so along with condemning Laodicea, this letter invites Laodicea to hope. Echoing several Old Testament prophets, Christ invites them: Come and buy from me real gold that has been purged of its corrupting power (see Jer 9:7; Zech 13:9; Mal 3:3). Come and buy from me real white robes to cover your shame. Come and buy from me real salve that will open the eyes of your hearts (3:18).

"Listen!" says the Christ to the lukewarm Laodiceans. "I am standing at the door, knocking; if you hear my voice and open the door, I will come in to you . . ." (3:20). In other words, he says, "I want to dwell among you, to give you what really matters, to have you live by my values. I want you to live a real life, not the false lives of the lukewarm."

This last of the seven letters ends in the grandeur of a promise: If you will open the door, I will come in. If you conquer, you will have a place with me "on my throne" (3:21). Then the summons that is now so familiar is repeated: "Let anyone who has an ear listen to what the Spirit is saying to the churches" (3:22). The point is utterly clear: Christ is not addressing only the church at Laodicea. He is addressing all the churches of all the years.

1. How do the letters to the seven churches set the stage for the rest of Revelation?

_____

_____

_____

_____

_____

2. Toward which of the churches do you have the most positive feelings and why?

_____

_____

_____

_____

_____

3. Toward which of the churches do you have the most negative feelings and why?

_____

_____

_____

_____

_____

4. What does it mean when Christ says to the church at Philadelphia that he has set an open door before them? Do you believe he has set an open door before you? If so, what is it?

_____

_____

_____

_____

_____

5. What is lukewarm about the church today?

_____
_____
_____
_____
_____

6. Which of the seven churches is most like yours? Why?

_____
_____
_____
_____
_____

7. Which of the letters is your favorite? What about it appeals to you?

_____
_____
_____
_____
_____

Come Up Here!

The opening verses of Revelation 4 are jarring. The letters to the seven churches are finished, and now John is suddenly in heaven seeing strange sights like emerald rainbows and creatures with too many horns and eyes. Chapter 4 is nothing like what we have just read. The subject matter changes. The style of writing changes. The mood changes. The scene changes. Everything changes. Why is there such an abrupt transition? Some think it is because a different author wrote the fourth chapter, but I believe there is a more natural explanation.

As we have seen, Revelation as a whole is a letter to seven local churches, and it begins logically with a specific letter to each of those churches. These seven short epistles inform us about the situation and the challenges of each church, and then the rest of Revelation speaks broadly to all of those situations and challenges. This makes the letters the key to understanding the remainder of Revelation. Everything that John is about to reveal is designed to give strength and hope to the churches as they struggle with persecution from without and inadequacy from within. The transition between these two sections is abrupt for a good reason: the contrast between earthly churches and a heavenly throne room is stark.

We should not miss the fact that the message to the seven churches is also intended for us. Seven is the number of completeness, and so the fact that there are seven churches suggests that Revelation speaks to the complete church. Yes, Revelation is addressed to seven little first-century churches that are trying to survive the Roman Empire (1:4), but it also addresses all churches, the complete church of God, that is, the complete church for which the Lamb was slain.

Chapters 4 and 5 provide for John a transitional period of worship between the letters to the churches and the release of God's judgments. Worship is the only context in which the coming judgments can be understood. Many readers, in my view, judge God too harshly for judging evil too harshly. Only in an attitude of worship can we hope to see the justice of his judgments. But before we look at Revelation 4 and 5 more carefully, let's summarize what John saw.

John begins this part of his vision by telling us that the voice of God trumpets an invitation into heaven as he says to John, "Come up here!" (4:1). John then passes through an open door and finds himself in the very presence of God. He was in God's presence in the worship experience on Patmos in chapter 1, but this time he worships in heaven, face to face with God and the heavenly host.

He discovers that he is in a different mode of existence here, one that he calls being "in the spirit" (4:1). By this, he means that he is totally immersed in God. He is no longer captive to the flesh or the world, but in this moment he has his whole existence in the spirit of God.

While in the spirit, John sees the beauty of God as he has never seen it before. That beauty, he says, is like the beauty of the precious stones jasper and carnelian. Above the throne of God, he sees a shimmering rainbow the color of an emerald. The throne itself is surrounded by twenty-four more thrones, on which sit twenty-four elders wearing white clothes and golden crowns. Lightning flashes around the throne, accompanied by the rumbling and clapping of thunder.

Seven torches burn, and "something like" a sea of glass lies before the throne as transparent as crystal. Four impressive living creatures are there, one like a lion, one like an ox, one with a face like a human, and one like an eagle. They can see everything, and they worship God day and night. In celestial chorus they sing, "Holy, holy, holy, the Lord God the Almighty, who was and is and is to come!" (4:8).

The twenty-four elders join the four living creatures and fall down and worship the "one who lives for ever and ever" (4:9). They cast their crowns before him, surrendering their own power, glory, and honor to the one who is Lord over all.

Then John focuses on the center of the scene. God holds in his right hand a scroll sealed with seven seals. No one is able to open this scroll. It is so full that the writing continues on the inside and the back of the parchment. John weeps because no one can open this scroll, but what he sees next alters this situation.

Between God and those who surround him is the Lion of the Tribe of Judah. Before John's eyes, the Lion becomes a Lamb. Paradoxically, the Lamb is alive, but it has been slain. It has seven horns and seven eyes, and it is, Revelation says, the seven spirits of God. Amazingly, this Lamb that was slain is able to open the scroll. He takes the sacred document in his hand, and when he does, all who are present fall down before him. Then the congregation of heaven brings him golden bowls of incense and sets them before him. As they offer these bowls to God, they sing a new song. The hosts of heaven sing, and then "every creature in heaven and on earth and under the earth and in the sea" (5:13). All worship him, and all give praise. The scroll is about to be opened; its mystery is about to be unveiled.

The Importance of Symbols

Now that we have the scene in our minds, obviously full of symbols, let's think for a moment about symbols and why they are used. This will help us later in the chapter as we discuss the meaning of the scene. It will also help us interpret the rest of Revelation, since from this point on the book is replete with symbols. Some of those symbols are bizarre and foreign, like the beast or the four living creatures. Others are comforting and hopeful, like the vision of God's throne room or the vision of the new Jerusalem coming down from God out of heaven. These symbols are powerful, and many are quite beautiful, but their occasional obscurity is one of the primary reasons so many people have trouble understanding Revelation.

First of all, symbols are by definition not literal truth. Many students of Revelation insist on interpreting it as literally as possible, believing that only the most obvious symbols should be understood as such. The book itself, however, tells us again and again that it is using symbols. A literalist style of interpretation leads us relentlessly toward mind-bending and often bizarre understandings of the Apocalypse that do not fit well with the God revealed by the rest of Scripture. The resulting effect is that, all too often, Revelation becomes simply a strange and exciting book that has little relevance to our lives.

This kind of interpretation would have shocked John of Patmos, who never intended that his letter should be read in this way. The other apocalypses of this period give us a clue as to what he intended. Apocalypses were not literal; they were highly symbolic documents. John's intention was to deliver a message specifically relevant to the needs of seven first-century churches in Asia Minor, with strong implications for the entire church of God. It was a message designed to encourage them and to steel them for ministry in adverse circumstances. It was a message sent from heaven, and as such it could not be communicated through the normal processes of language. It demanded poetic expression. Readers twenty centuries later interpreting his writing as a literal, physical description of what was about to happen would have been the last thing John expected.

Quantifiable language simply cannot communicate unquantifiable reality. This is the primary reason Revelation makes such heavy use of symbols. Symbolism is perhaps the form of expression best suited to communicating that reality that cannot be quantified. Symbols point to beyond themselves and are therefore not limited by the rational finite understandings of human minds. The symbols in Revelation convey impressions, glimpses of truth, that could never be conveyed through normal language. Symbolism does not, as some might fear, reduce Revelation to the level of fiction. It raises the book to a level of inspired spiritual insight that merits its place in the canon of Scripture. Revelation resists the temptation to whittle truth down to human size. Instead, it gives us what poet William Wordsworth termed "intimations of immortality."

Interpreting symbols, however, is a task so daunting that it dissuades many from even trying to understand Revelation. But for those who persist, the reward is a vision from heaven that has the power to sustain us through every trial of life. What is the secret to interpreting the symbols of Revelation? Symbols are elusive, and deciphering them is an inexact science. Still, a few principles can help us handle them with integrity.

First of all, symbols are fluid. Because they often represent the inexpressible, they cannot be pinned down too tightly to a single meaning. They may represent one thing in one context and something else in another. They may also have multiple meanings, even within the same context. They slip around on us. This should not be surprising, for symbolism is the language of mystery, not the language of science. If each symbol in Revelation had just one unchanging definition, then we could construct a glossary and simply look up the meaning of each passage. Of course, symbols do not work that way. If they did, they would be capable of telling us about nothing more than the realities we already know. They would lose their capacity to summon the unseen, to call forth the reality that lies beyond the veil of human thought and experience, and this was precisely what John was instructed to do.

Second, symbols are often allusions to other literature. Do you remember how hard it was to make sense of the poetry we read in high school or college? One of our problems was that many of its symbols were references to classical literature of which we knew little or nothing. We had to learn what the references pointed back to before we could learn what the poems meant. We have a similar problem when it comes to biblical symbols. Many images in Revelation are references to the writings of the Old Testament prophets, literature that is largely unfamiliar to us. The prophets' writings can be difficult reading in and of themselves, and so the allusions to them can be both obscure and ripe for unchallenged misinterpretation.

It is not uncommon for Revelation to lift symbols straight off the pages of the prophets. While John often gives somewhat different meanings to the images than the prophets did, we cannot understand his symbols if we do not understand what the prophets meant. During the course of our study, numerous examples will illustrate this point.

Finally, understanding symbols requires using our imaginations. The mind is not enough. Obviously, if the message of Revelation is too big for the mind alone, then we should not expect to grasp it with the mind alone. The imagination carries us beyond our rational minds. It allows us to apprehend realities that mere minds cannot grasp. Imagination is not the quality that allows us to create the imaginary. Instead, it is the language of the soul. Whenever we reduce the interpretation of Revelation to charts and graphs and codes, we miss the whole point of the book. We destroy mystery in a vain attempt to find understanding. If we are ever to understand Revelation, we must respect the mystery that lives in its symbols, for in that mystery is our hope.

Now we are ready to look more carefully at chapters 4 and 5. Chapter 4 may be regarded as a high expression of the beauty of God. Chapter 5 describes the great scroll and the Lamb who opens it.

Revelation 4: The Beauty of God

The "beauty of God" is a term that I have only learned to use in the last few years, but the fourth chapter of Revelation describes exactly that. The symbolism of chapters 4 and 5 becomes the exquisite vehicle by which John communicates the beauty of God. In the overview at the beginning of this chapter, we brushed by these symbols, but now we will consider briefly what at least some of them mean. We do not have the space to engage in a detailed analysis, but that will actually prove to be an advantage because it will keep us from getting so bogged down in each symbol that we miss the magnificent sweep of the whole. Revelation 4 is greater than the sum of its parts, and so, as we shall see, is chapter 5.

The first symbol to notice is the door to heaven. Through this door, John enters the mysteries heretofore unseen (and we enter through him). The most surprising thing about this door is not that it is there; the most surprising thing is that it is open. For all the ages, the leaders of Israel had spoken of the throne of God. They had gazed at the heavens and wondered about this door, but it had always been closed. Now, not only is the door open to John but he is also invited inside.

This door opens on a different reality, just as all doors do. But the reality on the other side of this door is not just a new room, the dusty cities of the seven churches, or rocky Patmos. This door opens to the heavenly realm. John describes it in ethereal terms, but it lies just beyond the door. It is closer than John, or any of us, could ever have imagined.

Once he passes through the door, John finds himself in a rich field of symbols. The most powerful one is the throne of God, that exalted symbol of God's ultimate power. God sits on a throne higher than Caesar's, and he presides over a court grander than Caesar's. This message was not lost on the seven churches. It was as though Revelation said to them, "The God you serve is mightier than the Caesar who commands your worship. The God you serve is the king of all the Caesars who ever lived."

The throne scene is breathtaking. God blazes like carnelian and jasper, precious stones used as symbols of his incredible beauty. A rainbow rests above the throne, shining like an emerald and reminding all who see it of the rainbow God gave to Noah as an abiding symbol of his mercy. The meaning for the churches is impossible to miss: in spite of all our failings, the final word from the throne of

God will be mercy. Twenty-four elders surround the throne, possibly representing the spiritually wise leaders of the church. They may be martyred and persecuted on earth, but in heaven they rule with God. Thunder and lightning accompany the presence of God, just as they did when God gave the Ten Commandments to Moses on Mt. Sinai. The seven torches burning in front of the throne, John tells us, symbolize the seven spirits of God. This does not mean that there are seven Gods. Rather, the number seven as a symbol for completeness points to the fullness (or "completeness") of the spirit of God. A sea that is like crystal lies before the throne. Its waters are not dark and murky, hiding the monsters that the ancients believe live there. Instead, the threatening sea is made as transparent as crystal, shimmering and reflecting the light of God. For the seven churches, whom chapter 13 describes as victims of the beast who came from the sea, the sea has lost its terror. The four living creatures who surround the throne are fraught with resemblances to angels described in both Isaiah and Ezekiel. The faith of their spiritual fathers and mothers has guided them to this day. At last, the assembly of heaven falls down before God and sings praises to him. These praises have inspired Christian music for two thousand years. Great hymns like "Holy, Holy, Holy" and "Worthy of Worship" and wonderful praise choruses like "He Is Worthy" are based on these words that the assembly of heaven sings. The church universal has always understood the message that was first given to the seven churches: although the world is full of tribulation, what began with the praise of God will end in the praise of God.

The cumulative force of these symbols makes Revelation 4 a powerful passage of Scripture. It is one of the most majestic descriptions of the wonder of God ever written. Read it aloud, and do not be surprised if the hair on the back of your neck stands up. Such is the descriptive capacity of symbolism.

The bottom line of John's paean of praise in chapter 4 is of course the beauty of God. Revelation as a book of visions is often associated only with darkness and doom and dragons and beasts, but it turns out to contain powerful and poetic visions of God's beauty.

John Keats's poem "Ode on a Grecian Urn" includes the famous lines, "Beauty is truth, truth beauty,—that is all / Ye know on earth, and all ye need to know." When I first became familiar with those lines many years ago, I was skeptical. It seemed to me that Keats was wrong and that truth was more than beauty. I suppose I was thinking of truth as fact and of beauty as ephemeral. But with the passing of the decades, my understanding of beauty and truth has deepened (or so I like to think). Much more now, I understand truth as more than facts, and I have beheld the beauty of God. I have beheld it in the eyes of the comforted, in the peace of healed hearts, in the compassion of the hopeful, in the subtle glory of the creation, and in the inestimable grandeur of the Word of God. All this has changed my mind. Now I believe that Keats was right. To behold God's beauty is truth, it is worship, and, as both John Keats and John of Patmos discovered, it is all we know on earth and all we need to know.

Revelation 5: The Scroll and the Lamb

There are two central symbols in chapter 5, the scroll and the Lamb. At the beginning of the chapter, the scroll appears: "Then I saw in the right hand of the one seated on the throne a scroll written on the inside and on the back, sealed with seven seals" (5:1). Some have speculated that this book was the Lamb's book of life, the book that contains the names of all those who are to be saved. That is an unlikely interpretation since this book apparently contains no names, but if it is not the Lamb's book of life, what is it?

As we will shortly see, the scroll contains the judgments that will occupy the bulk of the remainder of Revelation. When the seven seals are opened, God's judgment will fall on his enemies. The scroll then reveals what God intends to do about the situation of believers on earth, and it has the power to unleash those intentions. Because there is so much to say about God's purposes, the scroll is written "on the inside and on the back." At this point, however, no one is able open the scroll, not even one of the heavenly beings. The scroll is sealed with seven seals. In other words, it is completely secure. God's purposes will not be unleashed until it is time. John weeps because the seals cannot be opened; he deeply longs for the holy and gracious purposes of God to be accomplished.

A stunning surprise comes just as John is reduced to tears. One of the elders tells John to look and see "the Lion of the Tribe of Judah, the Root of David" (5:5), who stands between the throne of God and the rest of creation. This Lion of the Tribe of Judah is mentioned in both Genesis 49:9 and Isaiah 1, and the Jews had long understood this image as a reference to the Messiah (Beasley-Murray, 124). When they visualized their deliverer, this Lion was often the picture they had in their minds. He would come roaring, powerful and strong, and would conquer the beasts of their jungles. But when John sees the Lion before the throne of God, it changes its character before his eyes. He looks to see the Lion, but he sees a Lamb instead. The Lion of human expectation gave way to the Lamb of God, slain to atone for human sin. The text says the Lamb has seven horns and seven eyes (5:6). If the description were literal, this would be a thoroughly gruesome and frightening creature. The seven horns, in fact, are symbols of the Lamb's perfect strength, and the seven eyes are symbols of his perfect vision and his perfect wisdom.

The Lion-turned-Lamb then takes the scroll from the right hand of God. One by one, he begins to break the seals. The slain Lamb alone is able to unleash the cleansing and redeeming purposes of God.

Overwhelmed by the good news that the Lamb is able to break the seals, all heaven falls down in worship. The prayer of Amos is about to be answered (Amos 5:24) in ways that Amos never dreamed. Justice is about to roll down like waters. The seven churches were not put off by this, nor did the host of heaven wring their hands about the horrors of God's judgment. Modern people can hardly understand it. Our culture has so much denied the reality of evil and underestimated its power that many of us see injustice in God's judgments. The first-century church, however, understood evil as a force unto itself, and they lived with its effects on a daily basis. The fact that the Lion of the Tribe of Judah is about to wipe Satan and his followers from the earth struck them as justice. They were comforted by the promise of it. They knew that evil would push back against God's effort to destroy it and that this would bring even more terrible tribulations than they had already known, but that did not diminish the comforting power of Revelation. God's judgments were no cause for fear; they were cause for rejoicing. The people got the message: the victory of God is near.

The four living creatures and the twenty-four elders now fall before the Lamb. Each holds a harp and a golden bowl of incense, and with these they praise God. John tells us that the incense contains the prayers of the persecuted saints who had pleaded for this moment for so long. Finally, the great host of heaven begins to sing. They sing a new song. They sing of the worthiness of the Lamb and his victory won by death. "The old hymns" are powerful, but sometimes only a new song will do.

John hears the voices of thousands intoning, "Worthy is the Lamb that was slaughtered to receive power and wealth and honor and glory and blessing!" (5:11). The finest hymn singing I have ever heard was in the seminary chapel when I was a student. Nearly everyone could sing, and nearly everyone did. The rich harmony and deep tones of that chorus brought me so close to heaven that it is now my model for imagining the music that John heard on the day he was invited into heaven.

Then it was over. The worship ended. The four living creatures and the elders said, "Amen!" And they waited for what was coming next.

1. Describe in your words what John saw in chapters 4 and 5.

_____
_____
_____
_____
_____

2. What are the three greatest encounters with beauty that you have ever experienced? Was God present for you in a real way in those experiences? How?

_____
_____
_____
_____
_____

3. Describe the most beautiful worship experience you have ever had.

_____
_____
_____
_____
_____

4. Write a brief paragraph in which you try to describe the beauty of God.

_____
_____
_____
_____
_____

5. How might the idea of the beauty of God change the way you worship?

_____

_____

_____

_____

_____

6. How does the use of symbols enhance John's description of the heavenly court?

_____

_____

_____

_____

_____

7. What Old Testament references do you find in chapters 4 and 5? How do they influence your interpretation of Revelation?

_____

_____

_____

_____

_____

Now John's vision turns from the glories of heaven to images of plagues and suffering. The Lamb begins to open the seals one by one, and terrors pour out that have frightened readers for the last twenty centuries. The seven seals are the first of three rounds of judgments. The seals will be followed by seven trumpets and then seven bowls of God's judgment. These images will continue one after another until chapter 19. They make up the bulk of the book of Revelation, but they are not its bottom line.

Let's not get ahead of ourselves, though. For now, we will focus on the seven seals.

The First Four Seals (6:1-8)

As the first four seals are opened, the famous four horsemen of the apocalypse appear. The four horsemen have become a part of pop culture, turning up in movies and books and even sports. Knute Rockne's 1924 Notre Dame backfield, for instance, was called the four horsemen of Notre Dame. The mere mention of the mysterious riders sparks both questions and fears for many. As we shall see, however, the four horsemen are generally not well understood by those who turn them into pop images. We will examine them one by one, but let us first get an overview of the drama of the scene.

As the Lamb opens the first seal, all the heavenly host must be holding their collective breath. One of the four living creatures utters a single thunderous word: "Come!" And the first horse appears. Perfectly white, he carries on his back a rider holding a bow and a crown. Horse and rider, we are told, "came out conquering and to conquer" (6:2).

Then the Lamb breaks the second seal, and a second of the four living creatures summons another horse with the same thunderous "Come!" The second horse appears, and John explains that it is bright red. The rider of this horse bears a great sword and uses it to take peace from the earth, leaving in his wake human beings who slaughter one another like animals.

For a third time the Lamb opens a seal, and the third living creature utters the command again: "Come!" The third horse and rider suddenly come into view. This horse is as black as coal. Its horseman holds a pair of scales and speaks in puzzling phrases: "A quart of wheat for a day's pay, and three quarts of barley for a day's pay, but do not damage the oil and the wine!"

The Lamb then breaks the fourth seal, and the fourth of the living creatures calls out, "Come!" The horse appears, and it is pale green. The rider of this horse is the only one that has a name. His name is Death. Hades follows him, and together Death and Hades are "given authority over a fourth of the earth, to kill with sword, famine, and pestilence, and by the wild animals of the earth" (6:8).

The breathtaking horsemen ride together, gathering our imaginations and stirring our emotions. Their mystery makes us hunger to understand them.

The starting place for understanding is in the relatively unknown Old Testament book of Zechariah. In the first chapter of Zechariah's prophecy, he describes horses and riders similar to but not identical with the horses and riders of Revelation. Like John, Zechariah tells of four horsemen, but their colors are different from the colors of John's horses (Zech 1:7-11), and their mission may be as well. Zechariah says that these horsemen are God's patrol, sent out to determine the peaceful state of the earth. A few chapters later (Zech 6:1-8), Zechariah reports another vision in which he sees four chariots, each drawn by a different-colored team of horses. An angel tells him that these are the four winds of heaven, also sent out to patrol the four corners of the earth.

This message makes perfect sense for the time in which it was written. In Zechariah's day, Babylon had fallen to the Persian Empire, and the Persian king Cyrus had given permission for Jews who wished to do so to return to their homeland. Zechariah's prophecy seems to be God's way of saying to the returning Jews, "Do not be afraid. I have scouted the land and will secure it for you. All is in readiness for you to go home."

John's four horsemen at first appear to be quite different, and we are left to wonder if there is any connection between them and Zechariah's horse patrol. The four horsemen of Revelation deliver plagues and tribulations, and they do not appear to be securing the land like their counterparts in Zechariah. On the other hand, perhaps that is exactly what they are doing. Perhaps they are securing it for the return of Christ. As we move through our study, this interpretation will fit well. Tribulation seems to be a necessary prerequisite to the coming of the new Jerusalem.

The first horse, the white one, carries a rider who holds both a bow and a crown. Almost from the beginning, some have believed that he represents Christ going forth to conquer the world, but this interpretation simply does not fit. The other three riders are all about war and the consequences of war, and the rider of the white horse carries a bow, an instrument of war. In addition, chapters 6–19 are one long description of woes. It seems unlikely that the white would be the sole positive image in this whole section of Revelation. It is much more consistent with the context to understand the rider of the white horse as representing conquest (Caird, 80).

This makes even more sense when we consider that Israel had recently suffered the horrors of conquest at the hands of the both the Parthians and the Romans. In AD 62, the army of the Parthian Empire had invaded Israel in a war with Rome. They defeated Rome with the only mounted archers in the ancient world, all riding white horses. Eight years later (in AD 70), Rome extended its rule over Israel, brutally putting down a Jewish rebellion. In the process, they dismantled Israel and destroyed the temple itself.

The second horse also represents war. It is blazing red, the color of war. Its rider carries a great sword and possesses the power to take peace from the world. In the wake of his ride, this rider leaves human beings slaughtering one another like animals. This is, of course, the picture of war: the slaughter of the masses, the inhumanity of humans to other humans, and the absence of peace from the earth. War has, of course, always existed, and it will continue to exist until God defeats all such evils. The rider of the red horse represents the ultimate unleashing of all of war's horrors. His ride is consistent with Jesus' prediction that there will be "wars and rumors of wars" as the final days draw near (Matt 24:6).

The third horse is black, and the figure on its back carries a pair of scales. This horseman represents famine, one of the ugliest consequences of ancient wars. His scales are to weigh out food, and he weighs out precious little. He weighs out a quart of wheat on his scales, and a voice from the midst of the four living creatures says, "A quart of wheat for a day's pay!" (6:6). A quart of wheat was just enough to feed a person for a day, leaving him or her with nothing for other needs and nothing for tomorrow (*Interpreter's Bible*, 12:412). The horseman takes his scales once more and weighs out three quarts of barley. The voice speaks again and says, "three quarts of barley for a day's pay" (v. 6). Three quarts of barley was barely enough to feed a small family, and again for just a day. The third horseman rides away and leaves the earth in economic desperation, racked by famine, with barely enough to eat.

The voice continues, ". . . but do not damage the olive oil and the wine!" (v. 6). Ordinary people ate wheat and barley. The rich were the only ones who had ready access to olive oil and wine. The wealthy, in other words, give up nothing while others sacrifice everything. The rider of the black horse leaves behind him a world of injustice where the rich get richer and the poor barely eke out a living.

The last horse is a pale horse (or pale green as some translations have it). Its rider is Death. He and his partner Hades are authorized to use sword, famine, wild animals, and plague to wreak their fiendish power over a fourth of the earth. (This reference comes from Ezekiel 14:21, where Ezekiel refers to them as "four dreadful judgments.") This limitation of their power to a fourth of the earth means that the end has not arrived when the horsemen ride (Mounce, *What Are We Waiting For?*, 29). Death's powers are not fully unleashed; the sufferings of the horsemen come before the final battle between God and evil. The churches of John's day were familiar with the plague of Death. They had witnessed firsthand the terrors of Death and Hades. They had seen the ravages of war. They had known famine and pestilence.

All four horsemen have now ridden across the stage of Revelation: conquest, war, famine, and death. But why do they ride? What are we supposed to make of their appearance?

The meaning of the four horsemen can be understood at multiple levels. At the first level is the world of John's first readers. This would have been the most natural frame of reference for first-century Christians as they interpreted the horsemen. Their first thought would not have been that the four horsemen would ride in the distant future; they expected to see them in their own time.

They would have been quick to hear John describing woes they already had suffered. The hunger for conquest was already devouring their land.

The message of the four horsemen at this level was that even through the people's sufferings, God was achieving his final purpose. This gave suffering believers a reason to endure. Their faith was in the God who reigns over every circumstance.

At another level, the four riders have an apocalyptic meaning. After all, the horsemen are part of John's vision of things that "must take place after this" (4:1). They represent more than the sufferings of the past or even the present. They represent the sufferings of the future, the sufferings of the end of the age. These sufferings are necessary because, as the final victory approaches, the cosmic battle against evil rages ever hotter. They are endurable because they lead to victory.

On June 5, 1944, the night before D-Day, thousands upon thousands of military personnel trembled in fear of the suffering and death that awaited the next morning when they would cross the beaches of Normandy under German fire. Yet they knew that this fiery path was the only way to victory, and so they overcame their fears, and, as the morning light appeared, they flooded the beaches. Many gave their lives that day, but they had the courage to advance in spite of this because the invasion would open the pathway to victory. In the same way, the vision of the four horsemen encourages believers to forge ahead in the face of tribulation.

Revelation often presents dark pictures, but darkness must be faced. In this way, Revelation is a very realistic book. It does not shrink from the fact that evil must be confronted and totally exposed, or it can never be finally defeated. Only when sin is unmasked, only when it is seen in its frightening power, only when its ugliness is stripped bare can the final victory be won. Until then, the Prince of Darkness will continue recruiting and destroying those who are blind to what evil really is.

The Fifth and Sixth Seals (5:9-17)

As Christ breaks the fifth seal, a change of scene occurs. While the action revealed by the opening of the first four seals occurs on earth, the action revealed by the fifth occurs in heaven (Metzger, 59). The opening of this seal reveals the souls of the martyrs beneath the throne of God. The martyrs were of great concern to first-century believers. Many of them had seen with their own eyes the ruthless murders of the martyrs. They had witnessed or at least heard firsthand accounts of the cruelty that killed them and the agony in which they died. They cared deeply about those who had given everything for the faith, and they knew that the same might one day be required of them.

As John sees the souls of the martyrs, they cry out for vengeance but are told to wait a little longer. The end has not come. More will yet be martyred; more will yet be saved. Then justice will come, but only in its time. This message offers powerful comfort to the early church. Their martyrs have not been annihilated, but are safe beneath the throne of God. Justice is coming, and God will prevail. This message is grace for the followers of Christ in every time. In every period of history, saints have been slain for their faith. Their voices may no longer be heard on this earth, but they are safe with God, and his justice will come at last.

Then the sixth seal is opened, and another vision of truth appears. This is a vision of judgment and calamity, so that "the kings of the earth and the magnates and the generals and the rich and the powerful, and everyone, slave and free, hid in the caves and among the rocks of the mountains . . ." (6:15). In other words, all the kings who oppress Christians, all the cruel conquerors of all the ages, will be brought down from their mighty thrones. The kings of evil empires and the kings of realms of gold will all be brought to judgment before the King of kings.

The judgment of God reverberates from the breaking of this seal. The mighty of the earth are being destroyed, and so are all who are their partners (as indicated by the term "everyone" in Rev 6:15). A great earthquake shakes the earth, and the sun's face fades to utter blackness. The full moon becomes like blood, and the stars of the sky fall to the earth (6:13). The sky is "rolled up like a scroll," and every mountain and island is "removed from its place" (6:14). Obviously, these are not events that occur in the physical world. Stars cannot fall to earth; they are far too large. Besides, if they did fall to earth, they would consume the earth in an instant, and this is not what happens in Revelation 6. Stars falling on the earth can, however, give us an unforgettable spiritual image of God's wrath falling on his enemies. The catastrophes described here are drawn from the Old Testament, and they convey to us that every power on earth that opposes God will one day be defeated, and the enemies of God and his church will scramble to find a place to hide from his terrible wrath.

The Seals Interlude (7:1-17)

Before the opening of the seventh seal, there is an interlude in which John is shown two more visions. Similar interludes will occur later between the blowing of the sixth and seventh trumpets and between the sixth and seventh bowls. In each case, they provide reassurance to believers, relief from the intensity of the vision, and a heightened anticipation about what comes next. The two visions in this first interlude assure believers that they will be safe from the sufferings of God's judgment. These visions are strength for the journey. They are notes of grace in the cacophony of judgment. They make clear that the message of Revelation to Christ's followers is a message not of terror but of deliverance. It is a message of terror only to those who serve the Prince of Darkness.

The first of these two visions is the sealing of the 144,000. It opens with four angels holding back the four winds of the earth. These winds often wipe out everything in their paths, but they are held back while 144,000 are "sealed," or protected from the fury that is about to be unleashed.

Who are the 144,000? Are they, as some say, the converted Jewish Christians of the first century? Are they, as others say, Jews who will be saved at the end of time? Are they, as still others say, the martyrs who appear in white robes in Revelation 14:1? Or could they be the new Israel, the church? To answer these questions, it would be helpful to ask whether the number 144,000 is symbolic or literal.

The passage itself gives us some clues. First of all, the 144,000 are composed of 12,000 from each of the twelve tribes of Israel (Rev 7:4-8). John lists these tribes, but the list presents several problems. For starters, the twelve tribes no longer existed in the first century. Then the list itself is structured a bit oddly. The tribe of Dan, for instance, is not listed at all, while some tribes are listed that were actually just parts of other tribes. While the tribe of Judah is usually listed first, it is not so listed here.

These difficulties are puzzling, but they matter far less when we understand that John is not speaking of the twelve tribes of ancient Israel at all. Rather, he is speaking symbolically of the New Israel, the church. John uses the tribes to demonstrate that the church, the new Israel, is continuous with the old Israel. The church is not some strange new religion; it is a natural outgrowth of Judaism. The specific names of the tribes are not important. The point is that God has cared for his followers in the past, and he will continue to do that for those who have responded to the salvation he has given through Christ Jesus.

The number 144,000 is also symbolic. In Revelation, virtually every number stands for something. It would be out of character for John to use 144,000 as a literal number. Besides, a literal interpretation makes no sense theologically. If the head count of the people in John's vision was only 144,000, that would mean that God limits the number of people he will save. The rest of the New Testament affirms clearly that this is not the case. Twelve, of course, is one of the numbers indicating completeness, and so is one thousand. One hundred and forty-four thousand, then, is perfection squared. The New Israel is complete. All of you, the vision says, who are numbered among the people of God will be saved. Not one of you will be overlooked or left out. Every one of Christ's redeemed will be sealed and protected spiritually from the forces of evil in the great cosmic struggle. You need not fear Caesar's sword, the ravings of the Antichrist, or the mocking rejection of the world, even though you may have to experience them. You are protected by the power of God. They may persecute you and even kill you, but no enemy can finally destroy you. God will not forget you. He will not leave even one of you behind. You have suffered for the gospel. Now you are sealed, spiritually safe, awaiting the day of the Lord (Metzger, 61).

The second vision in the interlude answers some of our questions about the first. This is a vision of "the multitude that no one could count" (7:9). These people are not being sealed for the coming tribulation like the 144,000; they have already come through the tribulation (7:14). There are a multitude of them dressed in white, waving palm branches and singing praises to the one that sits on the throne. While they sing, one of the four elders asks John who they are. John replies that it is he (the elder) who knows. The elder tells John that the multitude is those who "have come out of the great ordeal" (7:14).

In other words, this multitude is the 144,000 on the other side of the great ordeal. The 144,000 and the number no one can count are the same. The only difference is that the 144,000 is a symbolic number used to communicate the completeness of the salvation of God, and the number that no one can count emphasizes the "magnitude of the multitude" who survive the tribulation. This multitude is not some small or exclusive group; it is the church. It is so large that no one can even imagine its number. All of these have come through "the great ordeal" (7:14) or, as other translations put it, "the great tribulation." Hope is not only for the few. It is for the masses.

The appearance of the term "great tribulation" in 7:14 raises questions for many readers, especially those who have been exposed to the teaching that the "Great Tribulation" is a seven-year period of intense trials that will immediately precede the return of Christ. This idea is based on the belief, first popularized in the early 1800s by an English interpreter named John Nelson Darby, that this Tribulation occurs as the last of the seventy weeks that Daniel prophesied in Daniel 9:24-27. While we do not have sufficient space to discuss that passage at length, suffice it to say here that several other interpretations of the Daniel passage understand his imagery to represent events that would occur much closer to his own time. If any of these other interpretations are correct, then the interpretation of the tribulation as a specific seven-year period would be impossible. Other interpreters believe the term "great tribulation" (not capitalized) refers to the tribulation of life or the tribulation experienced by the first-century church.

It surprises some people that Revelation 7:14 is the only place in the Bible where the term the "great tribulation" is used, but this is in fact the case. Even here, its precise meaning is somewhat unclear. Still, we can glean some clues to its meaning if we think carefully about the text of the entire book of Revelation.

One clue is that Revelation refers to present tribulation. The persecution of the first-century church is clearly intended in many of the images. The book itself begins with John calling attention to the persecution suffered by the seven churches and claiming that he too had been persecuted (1:9). The troubles of the early church are strongly akin to the troubles of churches in every century, and Revelation makes it clear that the Spirit is addressing all of those churches as a secondary audience to the original addressees of the book. In the last days, God will defeat all of these tribulations.

It is also true, however, that Revelation refers to the tribulation as an end-time event. For example, Christ says to the church at Philadelphia, ". . . I will keep you from the hour of trial that is coming on the whole world to test the inhabitants of the earth" (3:10). This coming hour of trial is among the things that are revealed to John when the voice in 4:1 says to him, "I will show you what must take place after this." Still, this end-time tribulation does not appear to be a phenomenon that introduces new forms of horror at the end of time. The devil we fight in the future will be the devil we know in the present. It is clear, though, that Revelation teaches that there will be a strong intensification of evil for a period at the end of time. In John's view, tribulation significantly worsens as God's battle against evil nears its end. Satan, the roaring lion, rages fiercest as the Lamb that was slain is about to slaughter him.

When John says that the numberless multitude has survived the great tribulation (the NRSV renders it the "great ordeal"), then, he offers hope to those who struggle with tribulations in the present and to those who experience the great final tribulation that is yet in the future. No Pollyanna, John says that even greater tribulation may lie ahead, but the greatest tribulation will be the suffering that comes just before the final victory. It will be the great darkness that comes just before the light. It will be the great confusion that comes just before all things are made clear.

The tribulation properly understood, then, is a message of hope. The second vision of the seals interlude ends when the elder who had explained the vision of the sixth seal assures John of the future of the saints who have endured: "They will hunger no more, and thirst no more; the sun will not strike them, nor any scorching heat; for the Lamb at the center of the throne will be their shepherd, and he will guide them to springs of the water of life, and God will wipe away every tear from their eye" (7:16-17). Those who see Revelation as nothing but a book of terror and judgment have misread the book.

The Seventh Seal (8:1-5)

At the end of the interlude, Christ breaks the seventh seal. When he does, we almost expect a clashing of cymbals and a storm of drums, announcing that the end of the prophecies of doom has at last come. This is not, however, what happens.

When the seventh seal is opened, there is simply silence. For the space of half an hour, everything is still. Only the breath of God could disturb this silence. We may never know with certainty the purpose of the silence, but it is natural. Whose tongue would not fall still after the display that has just occurred? We can speculate about the purpose of the silence. Perhaps it is to allow the numberless multitude to absorb what they have experienced. Perhaps it is to allow them to prepare for the blasts of the trumpets. Perhaps it is to allow God to hear the prayers offered by the saints. Or perhaps it is simply the silence of awe. All Revelation tells us is that it happened.

At the end of the silence, the seven angels receive seven trumpets. Waiting to blow them, they are now ready for the second act of this strange drama.

Before that second act begins, another angel appears. This one bears a golden censer and "a great quantity of incense" (8:3). As the aroma of the incense rises to heaven, it represents the prayers of the saints as they rise to God. British New Testament scholar George Beasley-Murray once said, ". . . it would seem that God has willed that the prayers of his people should be part of the process by which the kingdom comes" (151). That seems like an observation worthy of our reflection.

After the prayers are heard and the incense burned, the angel "took the censer and filled it with fire from the altar and threw it upon the earth; and there were peals of thunder, rumblings, flashes of lightning, and an earthquake" (8:5). The prayers of persecuted Christians contained in the golden censer are poured into God's heart. Then something more happens: God answers their prayers. He fills the empty censer with fire from the altar and pours out this fire in judgment upon the evil that persecutes his children.

Meanwhile, the angels with the seven trumpets stand by. Every ear in heaven is no doubt turned toward them, listening for the first note to sound. The trumpets are about to play.

1. What do each of the four horsemen of the apocalypse represent?

_____
_____
_____
_____
_____

2. What might the vision of the four horsemen have meant to first-century Christians?

_____
_____
_____
_____
_____

3. What might the four horsemen mean as an apocalyptic message for the end of time?

_____
_____
_____
_____
_____

4. Who were the martyrs, and why were they so significant to first-century Christians?

_____
_____
_____
_____
_____

5. The sixth seal shows destruction and calamity on the earth. Who is being destroyed?

_____

_____

_____

_____

_____

6. What are the two visions of the interlude, and what do they mean?

_____

_____

_____

_____

_____

7. Why do you think there was silence when the seventh seal was opened?

_____

_____

_____

_____

_____

8. If you were preaching a single sermon that interpreted all of the seven seals, what would be the point?

_____

_____

_____

_____

_____

The Seven Trumpets

Revelation 8:6–11:19

Divine judgment is never an end in itself. Though that judgment is about to be delivered once again, this time through the angels of the seven trumpets, it has two distinct purposes. First, the judgments warn the wicked of a greater judgment to come. Second, they call the wicked to repentance. The plagues of the seven trumpets are terrible, but they are not senseless. They are, interestingly, an answer to prayer, specifically the prayers of the saints that were delivered to God in a golden censer in 8:3-4. In response, God fills the censer with the fire of his judgment and sends it back to earth through the blasts of the seven trumpets. He does not send it simply to take vengeance on behalf of the saints. He sends it to begin the ending of human pain. To those who suffer, this is a message of hope because it is a reassurance that God will not abide their suffering forever.

The Opening Quartet (8:6-13)

The first four trumpets form a unit, just as the first four seals formed a unit. Each of the four announces similar plagues:

- The first trumpet: ". . . there came hail and fire, mixed with blood, and they were hurled to the earth; and a third of the earth was burned up, and a third of the trees were burned up, and all green grass was burned up" (8:7).
- The second trumpet: "Something like a great mountain, burning with fire, was thrown into the sea. A third of the sea became blood, and third of the living creatures in the sea died, and a third of the ships were destroyed" (8:8-9).

• The third trumpet: ". . . a great star fell from heaven, blazing like a torch, and it fell on a third of the rivers and on the springs of water. The name of the star is Wormwood. A third of the waters became wormwood, and many died from the water, because it was made bitter" (8:10).

• The fourth trumpet: ". . . a third of the sun was struck, and a third of the moon, and a third of the stars, so that a third of their light was darkened; a third of the day was kept from shining, and likewise the night" (8:12).

As is so often the case in Revelation, the images are strange to the modern ear. Perhaps if we were better students of the Old Testament, they might sound less strange to us, for much of this imagery originates in the Old Testament. The primary source of the images in the trumpet cycle is the book of Exodus. In fact, three of the first four trumpets release plagues that are similar to the plagues that fell on Egypt:

1. In Exodus, the Nile was turned to blood (Exod 7:14-25); in Revelation, the sea is turned to blood when the second trumpet blows (Rev 8:9).

2. In Exodus, thunder and hail fell on Egypt (Exod 9:13-35); in Revelation, thunder and hail fall when the first trumpet blows (Rev 8:7).

3. In Exodus, utter darkness falls on the land (Exod 10:21-29); in Revelation, utter darkness falls again when the fourth trumpet blows (Rev 8:12).

The fifth trumpet (which is not in the unit of four) echoes still another of the Exodus plagues. A plague of locusts fell on Egypt in Exodus 10:1-20; another plague of locusts falls on the land when the fifth trumpet blows in Revelation 9:3.

These parallels are too striking to be coincidental. It is clear that the Exodus plagues inspired this vision and helped its first-century readers to understand it. Knowing of the ancient plagues, the first readers of Revelation would have understood the vision to say that the same kind of judgment will fall on the enemies of the New Israel. The present may seem bleak and the persecution severe, but God's judgment is as sure in the future as it was in the past.

Still more Old Testament allusions are to be heard in the blasts of the trumpets. When the third angel blows, a star falls from the sky. The name of this star, Wormwood, is a reminder that in Jeremiah 9:15, God had said to a faithless Israel, "I will feed this people with wormwood and give them poisonous water to drink." Wormwood was extremely bitter to the taste. In John's vision, when the star Wormwood falls on a third of the rivers and springs, a third of the waters becomes bitter and kills masses of people (8:10-11).

Secular images from the first century are also detectable in this passage. For example, nearly everyone in John's world would have known of the eruption of Mt. Vesuvius and the ensuing destruction of Pompeii and Herculaneum. This had occurred just a few years before John wrote. When first-century believers read John's words saying that "something like a great mountain, burning with fire" was thrown into the sea (Rev 8:8), it would have been virtually impossible for them not to have thought of Vesuvius.

The fact that John's vision uses such familiar imagery is significant. Had he been describing a literal picture of the end of time, he would have had no reason to use images at all. He could have directly described what he saw. But these are images. John was once more using images of literal things to depict non-literal things. In addition, he was speaking to a specific audience, the seven churches. Images drawn from the Old Testament and from first-century events would have helped them understand what John was talking about. The vision he received was not meant to hide the truth; it was meant to reveal the truth. Personally, I have wrestled for many years with the literalist interpretation of Revelation that I learned in my youth, and I have come to believe that literalist thinking about Revelation actually leads us away from truth, not toward it. That is why I now believe that this kind of study of Revelation is so important.

Three key ideas about the meaning of the first four trumpets will help us understand them: (1) the sure advance of judgment, (2) the certain sound of warning, and (3) the holy hope of deliverance. Let's look at them one at a time.

The first idea is that the trumpets announce the sure advance of God's judgment. The first four trumpets step up the intensity of the judgments. In the judgments unleashed by the opening of the seals, for example, the fourth horseman (in Rev 6) was given power to kill one-fourth of those who live on the earth (Rev 6:8). Now, the fire burns a third of the earth, a third of the trees, and a third of all green grass (Rev 8:7). Furthermore, a third of the sea becomes blood, a third of the creatures in it die, and a third of the ships are destroyed

(8:8, 9). The star called Wormwood falls on a third of the rivers and fountains of water (8:10), and a third of the sun, a third of the moon, a third of the stars, and a third of the days and nights are utterly blackened (Rev 8:12). These "thirds" are intended not to convey exact mathematical precision but to convey that God is extending his judgment to extinguish ever larger portions of evil. The judgments of the trumpets have advanced, but they are preliminary and not final.

The second idea is that the trumpets are sounding a certain warning. Trumpets were often used as a warning call to repentance in ancient Israel (Caird, 108–109), and they are used in the same way in Revelation. The trumpet reveals the coming judgment and calls the wicked to repentance before the terror falls. Some read this as God threatening people into repenting. This is not how John sees it. He understands that God's judgment is necessary in order to end the evil that afflicts the world. In John's mind, the trumpets sound a warning of where evil inevitably leads and not the threat of a vengeful God. If we are to grasp John's message, we have to read his book on its own terms and not on the terms of twenty-first-century sensibilities.

The third idea is that the trumpet call is a call to deliverance. The notes of judgment played on the trumpets are grating, but this is not the only music the angels make. If we listen carefully to what lies beneath the text, we can hear grace notes playing as well. The trumpets sound notes of holy hope for a community long afflicted by the enemies of God. We have too often been deafened to these notes by the insensitivities of our own age, leading us to hear only the pain of judgment. The grace notes are playing nevertheless for those who have ears to hear "what the Spirit is saying to the churches."

That these grace notes are playing is confirmed by the grand service of worship that will follow the seventh trumpet in Revelation 11:15-19. The great joy of that worship reminds John's readers that all our tribulations are but for a little while. Ultimately, all tribulation will crumble before the sovereignty of God. The trumpets of Joshua's army heralded the collapse of Jericho's walls; the trumpets of Revelation herald the final collapse of the kingdom of evil. The sufferings revealed by the trumpets are not therefore the evil work of a sadistic God; they are the pains that are necessary in order for evil to die.

The Fifth and Sixth Trumpets (8:13–9:21)

Just before the last three trumpets blow, an eagle flies overhead crying, "Woe, woe, woe, to the inhabitants of the earth, at the blasts of the other trumpets that the three angels are about to blow" (8:13)! As we have learned to expect, deeper woes are about to afflict the earth. The first four woes of the trumpets came from the natural order. The last three come from supernatural forces of evil (Caird, 118). We will consider only the fifth and the sixth trumpets for now and leave the seventh for later. That, after all, is the way John has organized his book.

When the fifth trumpet blows, a star falls to earth and opens the shaft of "the bottomless pit" (9:2). Massive clouds of smoke pour from the pit and cover the sky with darkness. This is a sign that the dark face of the most demonic of forces is about to make its appearance. From the smoke come swarms of locusts, looking like scorpions and assembling as soldiers ready for battle. (Interestingly, at one stage of their development, locusts actually do resemble horses equipped for battle [Metzger, 64].) As mentioned earlier, the locusts are reminiscent of those that plagued Egypt so many years before. The locusts are allowed to inflict torture on those who do not bear the seal of Christ. God limits their curse to only five months, and he does not allow them to kill their victims. Instead, they leave their victims in agony, crying out to die but unable to do so.

The sixth trumpet also reveals supernatural forces of evil. A voice reverberates from the four horns (that is, the power) of God's altar, ordering the angel of the sixth trumpet to release "the four angels who are bound at the great river Euphrates" (9:14). The Euphrates is the eastern boundary of the Roman Empire. Those who live near it have become accustomed to fear. The river is the only physical barrier that protects them from the Parthian Empire and its armies to the east. When the four angels at the Euphrates are released, the protecting barrier of the river dissipates. Across that former border now swarms an army that dwarfs that of the Parthians. Two hundred million cavalry troops roar in upon them. This unimaginable army wreaks great devastation, killing a full one-third of humankind (9:18).

The meaning of the fifth and sixth trumpets—and, in fact, all the seals and the trumpets so far—is clarified at the conclusion of the plagues of the sixth trumpet: "The rest of humankind, who were not killed by these plagues, did not repent of the works of their hands of give up worshiping demons and idols of gold and silver and bronze and stone and wood, which cannot see or hear or walk. And they did not repent of their murders or their sorceries or their fornication or their thefts" (9:20-21). All the woes are sent to warn the hard-hearted to repent. Once again, to be warned is to be given mercy.

Many people are put off by a God who would allow a third of humanity to be killed simply to warn the wicked to repent. We live in a highly individualistic culture. In our minds, these people have done nothing to deserve the terrible fate that is meted out to them. We regard them almost personally. We react to the talk of their deaths as if they were our own. This kind of sensitivity was not characteristic of the ancient world, nor was it characteristic of John. Wars and plagues and death were facts of life. If God wanted to use these calamities for his purposes, then first-century people viewed that as his right. His ability to use an army of two hundred million to destroy their enemies demonstrated to them God's sovereignty, not his cruelty. For the first readers of Revelation, the bottom line of this vision was not slaughter; it was mercy and the opportunity for repentance.

If a third of the earth was slaughtered by the massive army, two-thirds survived. God had limited his wrath; but just as Pharaoh had hardened to the plagues that called him to repentance, the two-thirds harden to theirs. They prefer their own ways to repentance.

Few have ever been fully aware of the hardness of their own hearts, and most see no real reason to repent. In our age, as in every age, human beings tend to deify hard hearts, tough talk, and coercive action. We actually believe that this is the way to change the world. Jesus told us all along that the way was love instead.

The Trumpet Interlude (10:1–11:14)

An interlude follows the sixth trumpet, just as an interlude followed the sixth seal. Both serve the same essential purpose. They break the intensity of the narrative, and they provide reassurance to fearful believers. Both also contain two smaller visions. The two visions of the trumpet interlude are the vision of the little scroll and the vision of the two witnesses.

This vision begins with an angel descending from heaven, wrapped in a cloud that symbolizes God's presence. Above his head is a rainbow that symbolizes God's grace. The angel's face shines with the light of God's truth. His legs are likened to the pillar of fire that led the Israelites through the night after they escaped from the Egyptians. In his hand, this angel holds a little scroll, and he stands with one foot on the land and the other in the sea. This posture is a sign that the message in the little scroll is intended for the entire world.

The angel gives a great shout like a lion, and the seven thunders roar. Impressed, John starts to write down what he has heard, but a voice from heaven stops him. The judgments of the seven thunders are not to be written down. They will not be permitted to fall upon humanity.

Then the angel raises his right hand as if taking an oath, and he vows that there will be no more delay: when the seventh trumpet sounds, "the mystery of God will be fulfilled" (10:7). The fulfillment of that mystery has been delayed until this point so that people might have an opportunity to repent, but this reprieve is about to end. The final judgment is near. Of course, still more opportunities for repentance will occur in Revelation, leaving us to ask if the statement that there will be no more delay is in error. The statement is not in error. The explanation for this dilemma is that Revelation is not written in chronological order. It is not written in chronological order because it is not a book about the time sequence of the last days. The seals, the trumpets, and the bowls all speak of simultaneous realities. They do not provide a sequence of events for the end of time.

Next, the voice from heaven commands John to take the little scroll from the angel's hand and eat it. Of course, this is not to be understood as a command to John literally to eat the scroll. This would be impossible because the scroll itself is not literal; it is symbolic just as the larger scroll was. God wants John to devour the scroll in the same way that we would devour a book. That is, he wants John to make the message of the little scroll a part of himself. So John eats the scroll figuratively, and he finds it sweet to the taste but bitter to the stomach. The message of the scroll, as we shall soon see, is that the church has a mission. Any time God's people devour the word God sends to them, it demands a mission. When we first taste that mission, it is sweet, but when we actually undertake to do it, it can be bitter. It is sweet to sing powerful hymns that call us to service, and it is sweet to hear moving sermons that inspire us to action, but rejection and persecution are bitter medicine to take when we actually engage in the battle with evil ourselves.

By now, we are well aware that God's mission cost some first-century Christians their lives. Today, the list of martyrs is twenty centuries long. Christian pastors stood with their Jewish neighbors in Nazi Germany, and they were sent to the gas chambers along with the Jews. Christians in Darfur have held fast to their faith, and many of them have died. Martin Luther King, Jr., said to America that God had put a dream of equality and love in his heart, and he was fatally shot on a Memphis hotel balcony. Any time God's followers have opposed evil committed in the name of government or church or business, they have suffered, sometimes by defamation, sometimes by hatred, and occasionally by death. We should know this by now, for a voice from heaven told us long ago. When we praise God in our happy churches, it is sweet, but when we seriously apply it to a world of greed and pride and envy and hatred, not many of us have the stomach for it.

What, then, are the contents of the little scroll? As with nearly every verse in Revelation, many answers have been given, but one is especially obvious. The little scroll is to be understood in light of the larger scroll that came before it. If the larger scroll unveiled the purposes of God for the world, the smaller scroll unveils the purposes of God for the church. This is made clear in the command that John receives after he has eaten the little scroll: "You must prophesy again about many peoples and nations and languages and kings" (10:11). The little scroll is a mandate for the church to call human beings to faithfulness and repentance.

THE TWO WITNESSES (11:1-13)

A vision of two witnesses is the second vision in this interlude. In a brief preface, God instructs John to measure the temple but not to measure the court outside. Then God says, "I will grant my two witnesses authority to prophesy for one thousand two hundred sixty days, wearing sackcloth" (11:3).

What temple is to be measured? The temple in Jerusalem had been destroyed more than twenty years before Revelation was written. The word "temple" is used here to refer to the church. When God instructs John to measure this temple, he means that John is to put a protective boundary around the temple (the church), sealing it from its spiritual enemies. John was also told not to measure, or protect, the court outside the temple. That is where the nations dwell who are enemies of the people of God. Those nations, Revelation says, will trample over the temple, or the church, for three and a half years (11:2b). Several elements in the vision of the two witnesses need explanation. We will look at them one at a time.

The three and a half years. In a number of places, both Daniel and Revelation refer to a three-and-a-half-year period. These references have confounded readers for centuries and are the source of great debate among students of the Bible. Questions abound: Is this a reference to a literal period? Is it, as some say, the last three and a half years of Satan's reign? Is it the first half of a seven-year tribulation? Is it the first half of the seventieth week of Daniel's prophecy (Dan 9:24-27)? Or does it refer to something else altogether?

We must revisit the book of Daniel in order to answer these questions. At various places in his prophecy, Daniel refers to a period of three and a half years or, as he sometimes calls it, "time, times, and half a time" (see, for example, Dan 7:25; 12:7). The best scholars today believe that this period refers to a specific historical event that would have been familiar to the writer of the second half of Daniel.

When the second half of Daniel was written, Israel was under the rule of the Seleucid leader Antiochus IV. (While Daniel himself lived in the sixth century BC, the latter part of Daniel appears to have been written in the second century BC. Space prohibits a full discussion here, but the case for this position is strong.) The Israelites had tried unsuccessfully to overthrow Antiochus in a rebellion that became known as the Maccabean Revolt, and in retaliation he had decreed that the Jewish people must give up their national identity and their God and worship Zeus. For three and a half years, from 167 BC to 164 BC, Antiochus placed what Daniel called an "abomination of desolation" in the temple in Jerusalem. Whatever that abomination was, probably a Greek idol or possibly the profane offerings made in the temple, Daniel referred to it in three places (Dan 9:27; 11:31; and 12:7), and saw it as a defilement of Israel's holiest place. The abomination outraged the Jewish people. After the abomination was removed, three and a half years became a common apocalyptic image for times of Gentile domination or intense persecution (Metzger, 69). In Matthew, Mark, and Luke, Jesus also uses the abomination as an apocalyptic image.

Therefore, when the early Jewish Christians read in Revelation that the temple would be trampled for "three and a half years," they would have readily remembered that Antiochus's abomination had defiled the temple for three and a half long years. At the same time, they would have had enough perspective by then to know that three and a half years turned out to be a relatively brief period. They would have gotten the point that so often eludes us: although the persecution they were undergoing seemed to be lasting forever, God in his time would bring it to an end. Symbols, you remember, are fluid. John's vision speaks to first-century readers but also to all readers. All their tribulations, especially the huge one that lies ahead, will soon be over. They are not forever; their end is coming soon. God will one day raise his hand and say, "Enough!"

The olive trees and the lampstands (11:4-6). During the three-and-a-half-year trampling of the church that John sees in his vision, two witnesses are sent to prophesy. John likens them to two olive trees and two lampstands (11:4). The olive trees come from an image in the book of Zechariah in which they represented Zerubbabel the King and Joshua the priest (Zech 4:11-14). Revelation Christianizes the olive trees and lampstands and uses both images to symbolize Christ, since he is both King and high priest. The image of the lampstands refers to Revelation 1:12, where they represent the church. The two witnesses then are both olive trees and lampstands. Their identity is not a mystery. They are Christ and his church. In the last dark days of tribulation, Christ and the church will be there to bear witness to God's hope.

We might wonder why there are two witnesses. Aside from the obvious fact that Christ and the church are two, G. B. Caird offers the interesting observation that the testimony of only one witness was not admissible in Jewish courts (135). Two witnesses were required to validate a truth, as prescribed in Deuteronomy 19:15. The testimony of both Christ and the church reinforce one another and give undeniable credence to the gospel.

The Antichrist. The two witnesses have special protection. They are able to consume their enemies. They are able to command the sky and the waters and the earth. In spite of this, "the beast that comes up from the bottomless pit" (11:7) kills them and leaves their dead bodies lying in the street. Only the beast, the supernatural power of evil, is strong enough to do this. Yet even the beast can fulfill his evil mission only because he has been released from the pit by a power from above in the form of a falling star (9:1-2). His success, however, turns out to be short-lived. The bodies of the witnesses lie in the street for three and half days (11:8). Then they are raised from the dead.

Many refer to this beast, or to similar images in Revelation, as "the Antichrist." The word "Antichrist," however, appears nowhere in the book of Revelation. In fact, in the entire Bible it appears only three times, all in 1 and 2 John. First John 2:22 says that the antichrist is anyone who denies that Jesus is the Christ. This certainly justifies calling the beast the antichrist. His whole purpose in this passage is to stop the two witnesses who are proclaiming the Christian message. But we must be careful to remember that "antichrist" is not just one being in Scripture. Antichrist, according to 1 John, is anyone who denies that Jesus is the Christ. In fact, 1 John says that the spirit of antichrist is not just a beast coming in the future; it is already a present reality (1 John 4:3). Relegating "the antichrist" to the future is dangerous theology. It allows the spirit of antichrist to stalk us in the present with impunity, since he has no fear of being recognized. Revelation indicates that the power of antichrist grows stronger as his defeat approaches. He even has power over Christ and his church, but his victory will not endure.

God's unrelenting power prevails: "the breath of life from God entered them" (11:11). The bodies of the witnesses lie still in death for a mere three and a half days. Then their bodies throb with life again. The message to oppressed believers is strong: "God will not be defeated. Death cannot destroy his witnesses. The Word of God cannot be silenced. The beast may bring his slaughter, but through this slaughter God gives life to his Lamb and to his church."

The Rapture. The word "rapture" is common in theories about the end of time, but it does not appear a single time in Revelation. That means that there is no natural place for us to discuss it when we are studying Revelation, but since some think that the phrase, "Come up here!" (11:12) is a reference to the rapture, this is as good a place as any to consider it.

The rapture, as understood by many Christians, is an event at the end of time in which all Christians living and dead meet Christ in the air to be taken to dwell eternally with him in heaven. Many Christians believe that the rapture will be followed immediately by a seven-year tribulation such as was discussed above. Only those who are left behind will experience the tribulation. This is the pervasive view in our society, fueled by fiery preachers and a plethora of books, most recently the Left Behind series by Tim LaHaye and

Jerry Jenkins. Before we buy in to this understanding, however, it would be good to look at what the Bible says and does not say about the rapture.

Beginning with the passage at hand, the two witnesses are summoned into heaven at the end of the vision with the words "Come up here!" (11:12). The same words occur in Revelation 4:12. Many interpreters believe that both of these references are summons to the rapture. That these two verses refer to the rapture is a bizarre claim. In chapter 4, the words are plainly addressed only to John. In chapter 11, they are clearly addressed only to the martyrs. In neither case are they addressed to the whole church, and neither refers to a general resurrection. When we claim that the Bible means what the Bible does not say, we are walking on thin ice.

Not only does the word "rapture" not appear in Revelation; it does not appear anywhere in the Bible. There is a basis for the idea of the rapture in 1 Thessalonians 4:17-18, which says, "Then we who are alive, who are left, will be caught up in the clouds together with them to meet the Lord in the air; and so we will be with the Lord forever. Therefore encourage one another with these words." These verses clearly express a belief that when Christ returns, he will raise those who are dead in Christ and will gather his faithful who are alive at the return of Christ.

First Thessalonians, however, does not place these events in any kind of sequence, much less the one that is accepted carte blanche in the Left Behind books. In the dispensationalist theology on which these books are based, Jesus returns, the church is raptured up to heaven, and unbelievers are "left behind" to suffer seven years of tribulation before Jesus comes for yet a third time to usher in his kingdom. In fact, this sequence is not found explicitly recorded anywhere in Scripture. The second coming is a clear teaching of the New Testament, but not the Third Coming. Neither does Scripture say that the tribulation follows the rapture. The purported scriptural support for this sequence is drawn from piecing together various fragments of Scripture, but there is no conclusive evidence for this. If God had intended to communicate such an important teaching, I do not believe he would have buried it in a connect-the-dots puzzle.

Matthew 24:39-42 has often been cited as a passage that confirms the dispensationalist sequencing of the rapture. This is the passage (along with Luke 17:34-35) that says two will be in the field and only one will be left, two will be grinding at the mill and only one will be left. It sounds a lot like the rapture, but with one huge difference: the sinners in this passage are not left behind at all. In fact, they are the ones who are taken. And the saved are not the ones who are taken; they are the ones who are left behind. In fact, Jesus adds that in the days of Noah, the evil were swept away by the flood, and that in the days of the Son of Man they will be swept away again, this time forever. This passage simply does not contain the sequencing of the rapture and the tribulation that is taught by our traditional understanding of end-time events.

If this seems confusing, another verse from Matthew 24:36 may help. This verse says, "But about that day and hour no one knows, neither the angels of heaven nor the Son, but only the Father." This verse says not only that no one knows the specific time of Christ's return but also that no one has knowledge about this day and hour. In short, Jesus' return is taught by the New Testament, but the details are intended to be a mystery. Those who believe that God has revealed the timetable of the final days in coded languages and obscure references are quite at odds with Jesus. Paul beautifully expressed the point Jesus made: "For now we see in a mirror, dimly, but then we will see face to face" (1 Cor 13:12).

The Seventh Trumpet (11:15-19)

The last of the seven angels now blows his trumpet. He plays a surprising note. This note, like the contents of the seventh seal before it, leads not to another judgment but to worship. When the trumpet blows, loud voices in heaven sing to the One who has decimated all evil kingdoms and is about to end all human suffering forever. They sing the words that inspired Handel as he wrote *Messiah*: "The kingdom of the world has become the kingdom of our Lord and of his Messiah, and he will reign forever and ever" (11:15).

Then the twenty-four elders fall on their faces and sing the praises of God, saying, ". . . you have taken your great power and begun to reign" (11:17). They praise God for his judgments, his power, and his imminent victory over all those who had brought so much suffering upon the world. The judgments that have now been unleashed by the seven trumpets prove to be judgments not to fear, but to celebrate. For the faithful, these judgments are deliverance from evil. "The nations raged" (11:18), we are told, and what else would we expect them to do? The suffering of the good is about to end. No wonder the saints give praise.

Then, amazingly, from the mists of history, the ark of the covenant appears (11:19). This was the chest into which the Ten Commandments were placed in the time of Moses, the chest that accompanied Israel to the promised land, the chest that was lodged in the holy of holies in the temple in Jerusalem. Lost at the time of the Babylonian captivity, the lost ark turns out not to be lost at all. It has been hidden in the mystery of the ages, but it is now unveiled again as the lasting symbol of the presence of God. He who was with Moses is with us. The saints had wailed, "How long, O Lord, how long?" The seventh trumpet delivers the answer: "Now, my children. Now."

1. Why do the seven trumpets blow? What is God's purpose for sending their afflictions?

_____

_____

_____

_____

_____

2. What does it mean that John's vision includes four plagues so similar to the ones on Egypt in Moses' time? Which ones are most like the plagues on Egypt?

_____

_____

_____

_____

_____

3. What is the meaning of the little scroll?

_____

_____

_____

_____

_____

4. What have you learned about the Old Testament background of the three and a half years?

_____

_____

_____

_____

_____

5. What is the source of evil in Revelation? God? Satan? The synagogue? The Roman Empire?

_____

_____

_____

_____

_____

6. Who is the antichrist? What forces in the world today may represent the spirit of antichrist?

_____

_____

_____

_____

_____

7. Who are the two witnesses in chapter 11?

_____

_____

_____

_____

_____

8. What do you believe the Bible teaches about the rapture? What specific passages are the source of your belief?

_____

_____

_____

_____

_____

Conflict between the Church and the Powers of Evil

Revelation 12–14

Since the letters to the seven churches, John's visions have unfolded in an easy-to-follow outline: first there was the great worship experience in heaven, then the opening of the seven seals, and then the blasts of the seven trumpets. We might expect the seven bowls to follow immediately, but instead chapters 12–14 serve as a grand parenthesis describing the conflict between the church and the powers of evil. Some may see this as a digression rather than a parenthesis (a digression is only weakly connected to the surrounding text), but they would be wrong. The parenthesis prepares the reader for what is to follow. It addresses a question many Christians were no doubt asking: "Why must we wait? If we are the redeemed, why are we suffering like this?" It is the same question we are asking today. Why is evil allowed to have so much power in the world? When will it ever end? Chapters 12–14 deal with the problem of evil, the most daunting problem of the entire Bible and, arguably, of human existence. Like all of Revelation, this parenthesis is a message for every age, especially the last age. But in our eagerness to understand what these chapters mean for the end time, we must not ignore the fact that its message is also for us.

Chapters 12–14 contain three vivid visions. The first is the vision of the dragon and the woman giving birth (ch. 12). The second is the vision of the two beasts (ch. 13). And the third is a vision to give assurance to believers (ch. 14). Let's look at each of them in turn.

The Fearsome Dragon (Rev 12)

In the first chapter of this grand parenthesis, John tells of his vision of an ominous dragon. After we summarize chapter 12 briefly, we will talk about what it means.

First, John sees a woman "in the agony of giving birth" (12:2b). She wears a crown made of a dozen stars, and she is "clothed by the sun" (12:1). The moon lies beneath her feet. Before her stands a red dragon with seven heads and ten horns and seven diadems arrayed on his heads. With his powerful tail, he sweeps a third of the stars from the heavens, throws them to the earth, and waits for the woman to give birth so that he can devour her child. He wants to devour the infant because that infant is destined to be the ruler of all the nations, and he is therefore a great threat to the dragon. The instant the child is born, however, he is snatched from his mother and taken to be with God. The mother flees into the wilderness, and there God nourishes her for 1260 days, or three and a half years, a length of time by now familiar to us.

Then war breaks out in heaven as the dragon (Satan, as v. 9 tells us) and his hellish followers attack the archangel Michael and his heavenly angels. Michael's forces finally prevail, and the dragon is thrown down to the earth. A loud voice from heaven announces that Satan the great accuser has been defeated. He can no longer accuse God's children in the court of heaven; he can now tell his lies only on earth. Nevertheless, the final victory has begun. The voice speaks on and tells us that the dragon's defeat has been wrought not by any mighty weapons but by "the blood of the Lamb" (12:11). Heaven may now rejoice, for the victory there is won; but earth will still cry out, because the deceiver has come down in great wrath. His wrath is so great "because he knows that his time is short!" (12:12).

In a blind rage, the dragon now pursues the woman into a wilderness place that God has prepared for her. From his mouth, the dragon pours out a river of water to drown her, but God's earth opens its mouth and swallows the water. Then, in a telling phrase, John states that the dragon goes off to make war "on the rest of her children, those who keep the commandments of God, and hold the testimony of Jesus" (12:17). The woman is nourished by God until the time of the dragon is over.

That is the summary, but what does it all mean? For purposes of this discussion, we will examine two parts of the vision separately, first dealing with the birth of the child (12:1-6), and then with the

war in heaven and the dragon's pursuit of the woman (12:7-17). In each part, we'll talk first about what the major symbols mean, and then we'll talk about the overall meaning of the passage.

PART 1 (vv. 1-6)

The woman giving birth obviously refers to Mary at the birth of Jesus. This woman, however, is not simply Mary; she is the nation of Israel. Isaiah spoke of Israel in just this way (Isa 26:18). Also, the first-century Christian community known as Qumran produced writings that use this image. John, however, sees both the old and the new Israel in this woman giving birth (Beasley-Murray, 198). The old Israel had awaited him and labored to give him birth. The new Israel had suffered the birth pangs, nourished him and his teachings, and experienced persecution and rejection in order to follow him. In a real sense, the community of faith gives birth to the Messiah.

The dragon is another important symbol. Once again John wants to be sure we do not miss seeing who this dragon is, so he tells us in verse 9 that the dragon is Satan. Of course, this is confirmation from John himself that the images in this vision are symbolic. Satan appears as a dragon; in reality he is God's great enemy of the ages. Satan had tried to devour the infant Savior through the treachery of Herod. He had used unbelievers to attempt to destroy Jesus' ministry and his message. And at the end, he had used both Jewish and Roman authorities to send Jesus to the cross.

Seven crowns rest on the dragon's seven heads, reminding every reader that Satan often comes dressed in the garb of rulers. Human power is often used for good, hence Romans 13 tells us that the authorities that exist are instituted by God, but human power is too easily corrupted by the powers of darkness. This is seen again and again in the pages of both the Old and New Testaments.

The dragon's ten horns are reminders of his tremendous power, demonstrated dramatically as he wipes a third of the stars from the sky with a single swipe of his tail. In my view, the great theological error of our time is that we underestimate the power of evil. Perhaps this is why we moderns so easily dismiss the existence of the devil. The Bible is much more realistic. Evil is no merely human power. It has a name, Satan. It has an existence of its own. As Paul said, "For our struggle is not against enemies of blood and flesh, but against the rulers, against the authorities, against the cosmic powers of this present darkness, against the spiritual forces of evil in the heavenly places" (Eph 6:12).

As powerful as Satan is, however, he is no match for God. The instant the child is born, God snatches him away to protect him for his saving mission. God also prepares a place to nurture the church (the woman) while Satan vents his rage upon the earth for "three and a half years." Satan pursues the church into the wilderness, but God causes the earth to open its jaws and swallow Satan's threatening waters. The church emerges not only intact and alive but also nourished and strengthened. She is *more* ready for the service of God because she is persecuted. Again, as the second-century theologian Tertullian said, "The blood of the martyrs is the seed of the church" (*Apologeticus* 50).

This vision contains a message that is nothing short of overwhelming. It offers profound reassurance to first-century Christians that their lives were in Christ and could never be extinguished. Wild animals may have silenced some of them before roaring crowds, but no beast would ever silence the voice of the church. Flames of fire may have consumed the bodies of martyrs, but the flames of God's judgment would consume the wicked forever. The Roman Empire may have tried to eradicate them, but the Roman Empire, like the dragon himself, would only endure for a time. The dragon cannot destroy them. His days are short, and while he walks the earth God will hold his children in his hands.

To twenty-first-century western Christians, the vision offers a similar word: The culture may be abandoning your churches. Partisan politicians may have taken the gospel hostage. Society may no longer give you its respect. Lone-ranger spirituality may threaten the existence of your churches. The landscape of your ministry may be fierce and hostile like a wilderness. But in those barren places, God gives strength for our task and deliverance from our enemies. God who is mighty will sustain us and preserve us until the day of victory. Those who predict the death of the church have missed the vision of John and, in his view, believed the deception of the father of lies.

PART 2 (vv. 7-17)

Now John sees a war in heaven. This is not at all what we expect. Heaven is supposed to be a place of eternal peace where goodness prevails. How could there be war in heaven?

War comes to heaven only because the dragon brings it. He is not timid. With his followers behind him, he storms the gates of heaven. John sees clearly that this dragon, the devil, is so malevolent, so thoroughly evil, that he will even attack the holy habitation of God. As we have already seen, however, Satan's power is insufficient. Michael and his army of angels win the victory and throw him down to earth.

Such images of war do not sit well with all Christians today. Some churches now decline to sing hymns with war imagery. Hymns like "Onward Christian Soldiers" and "The Battle Hymn of the Republic" are shelved in favor of hymns with more pacific lyrics. John, interestingly, has no qualms about this kind of imagery. He uses it boldly, as though only warlike imagery were powerful enough to describe the intensity of the conflict between God and his enemies. To be sure, struggles between virtue and vice, between love and indifference, between our best selves and our worst selves, between God and the devil are not benign contests. They are nothing less than fights to the death. They are terminal struggles with the superhuman force of evil known as the devil. In John's vision, the victory is not to be won through some evolutionary process in which people gradually morph into Christ-like beings and in which society gradually morphs into the kingdom of God. It is to be won by the magnificent fury of God as he defeats the raging devil, the poisonous serpent, the father of lies, and the author of death. Revelation never wanders far from images of war and violence. From the four horsemen of the apocalypse to the battle of Armageddon, the war motif is ever present, a constant reminder of the deadly seriousness of the struggle between good and evil.

The defeat of Satan in his assault on heaven is significant because it is a harbinger of his defeat on earth. He may still vent his rage upon the earth, but now that he has lost heaven, his ultimate defeat is imminent. Also, in the book of Job he played the role of prosecuting attorney. Now that he is cast out of heaven, he can never again play that role.

This then is Revelation's response to the question of why Christians suffer: it is only a little while until Satan will be crushed. Soon and very soon, there will be no more suffering. This is not an explanation that satisfies the philosophers. It leaves too many questions unanswered. Where did Satan come from? Was it God who created him? Why was Satan cast to the earth after the battle instead of being utterly destroyed right then? Why is it taking God so long to win the victory against evil and bring down his justice on history? Centuries of philosophical reflection have left us without any satisfactory answers to these questions about evil and without any real strength to deal with that evil. But the answer to the problem of evil as given in Revelation is not a philosophical answer. It is a spiritual answer. A philosophical explanation might satisfy the mind, but a spiritual answer satisfies the soul. Because Satan's time is short, believers can endure his sting (12:12). God's purpose here is not to satisfy intellectual curiosity. It is to steel the church for the tribulation of its existence.

After Satan is defeated in heaven, the "loud voice" speaks again and says, "Now have come the salvation and the power and the kingdom of our God and the authority of his Messiah" (12:10). Then this exuberant declaration gives way to another warning and another hope: "But woe to the earth and the sea, for the devil has come down to you with great wrath, because he knows that his time is short!" (Rev 12:12). The warning, of course, is simply that the devil still inhabits the earth. The hope, as we have already discussed, is the promise that his time is short.

By now we know that the message of chapter 12 is that victory is assured. This message falls on the ears of a shaken first-century church. They have put their faith in Christ, but nothing has gone right. Rome has trampled them. The churches in Rome are hidden in catacombs, and churches everywhere are hidden in fear. Some Christians wonder if the faith will die in its infancy. All they know about the future is that it does not look good. Then they hear John telling them of his powerful vision. Satan has been thrown out of heaven. He tries to destroy the church on earth, but God protects his church in a place he has prepared in the wilderness. In that wilderness place, Revelation 12 says, he nurtures the church for its mission and keeps it until Satan and his evil kingdom are destroyed.

I once knew a woman who believed that God asked every morning, "What can I do to hurt this woman today?" She had lost her son in an automobile accident many years before and had been angry at God ever since. Well, there is someone who asks every morning what he can do to harm us, but Revelation 12 assures us that it is not God. The one who would harm us is God's great enemy, the devil. God is the one who gives us strength to endure, just as he gave it to the woman in the wilderness. Even now, he makes ready to crush forever the dragon of our afflictions.

The dragon is a potent symbol, and we will miss much of its meaning if we try to interpret it as a literal beast. G. K. Chesterton helps us understand with a comment he once made about fairy tales: "Fairy tales," he said, "are more than true; not because they tell us that dragons exist, but because they tell us that dragons can be beaten" (quoted by Neil Gaiman in *Coraline*, 2004). Revelation, of course, is not a fairy tale, but Chesterton's statement still applies. Revelation does not tell us that dragons exist; it tells us that the great dragon Satan can be beaten.

The Two Beasts (Rev 13)

The dragon does not work alone; he has minions. Two beasts come to his aid in chapter 13, one from the land and one from the sea. These beasts are intended not to frighten but "to call for the endurance and faith of the saints" (13:9).

Like most symbols in Revelation, the beasts are fluid images. That is, they represent more than one reality. At the most basic level, the first beast is clearly Rome. Like the Roman ships that bore soldiers and sometimes envoys, he comes from the sea. He makes "war on the saints and to conquer them" (13:7), just as the Romans had done. He commands the worship of all the people of the earth (13:4), just as Caesar had done. He has seven heads, just as Rome had seven hills. He has ten horns, just as Rome had ten emperors. On his head sit ten diadems, reminding first-century readers that Rome ruled over many nations. On one of his heads is a scar, a wound that had been healed, just as Nero's reign had left a scar on Rome. The symbolism here is not difficult to understand. Rome derived its terrible authority from Satan himself, the vision claims, just as the beast derived his from the dragon who represented Satan (12:9).

At another level, it is clear that this first beast represents something more than just Rome. The symbols are vague enough to be subject to other interpretations. In every age, different historical figures have been identified as the beast. The Pope, Stalin, Hitler, and a host of others have been so "honored." Most of us assume that this constant re-identification of the beast means that interpreters have not known what they were talking about. I do not believe this is the case. The beast, like its ruler the dragon, manifests itself in every age. The beast is every earthly power that serves the dragon. Later in Revelation, it will become clear that the beast will make himself known with virulent force in the final days. The father of lies and his minions are far too deceitful to be confined to a single historical figure or to any particular time.

Many observers have noted that the dragon and his two beasts form a kind of unholy trinity, absolutely opposed to the Holy Trinity but deceitfully resembling it. The dragon is the unholy counterpart of God. The first beast, having been healed from a mortal blow (13:3) like the Christ, is the counterpart of the Son. The second beast, being at work in the daily lives of the early believers, is the counterpart of the Holy Spirit. In this dragon's trinity, the unholy is disguised as the holy. That is why it is so easy to mistake evil for good and to presume that the Antichrist is the Christ.

The beast nearly succeeds in passing for God. Referring to Caesar, Revelation 13:8 says, "all the inhabitants of the earth" regard him as a deity and worship him. Roman emperors had been called gods since the time of Julius Caesar, but now Domitian built temples to the emperor and demanded that subjects address him as "our lord and god" (Metzger, 75). Millions who were under Roman rule had bowed their knees to worship the emperors. Revelation minces no words: a nation or a ruler that demands first place in the hearts of its people is nothing more than a beast under the sway of Satan.

Government is ordained of God, Paul said in Romans 13, but Revelation makes it clear that Christians are forbidden to give unquestioning loyalty to a nation or an empire. This type of commitment belongs only to God. Revelation makes this clear in the strongest of terms. The God of Revelation knew that nations and empires easily become beasts. They are easily taken captive by the dragon. The Roman Empire itself was relatively beneficent as a world power, allowing its conquered peoples a measure of freedom and ensuring their peace, and yet this empire was corrupted by the devil and became an instrument by which he fought the church. Most of its citizens were unaware of what had happened. They still saw Rome as good and gave it their unquestioning allegiance. John saw it for the beast it was.

Any nation, no matter how virtuous, is in constant danger of corruption. The dragon lusts to have the nations in his service, and so he often hijacks them for evil while their citizens remain trustingly unaware. Any nation that has been deified, any nation that has taken the place of God in the hearts of its people, is vulnerable to the powers of evil. Patriotism is a noble virtue. It makes a people strong. But Christian patriots must always take care, for the step from patriotism to idolatry is short. The Romans stepped over the line, and their empire turned into a beast that raged against God. Christians suffered at their hands, and through John's vision of the beast, God warned them of what was happening. At the end of the vision, he told them exactly why he had given it to John: "Here is a call for the endurance and faith of the saints" (13:10).

The second beast comes not from the sea but from the earth (13:11), that is, from the land where the seven churches ministered and lived. For this reason (and others that will become apparent in subsequent paragraphs), quite a number of Bible scholars believe that he represents the local presence of the Roman Empire.

The second beast resembles Jesus in several ways: he has two horns "like a lamb" (13:11), calling to mind "the lamb that was slain"; he wields authority on the authority of another; and he performs miracles. This resemblance, however, is deceptive. When the beast with two horns "like a lamb" speaks, he reveals his real identity as a destroying dragon. The beast derives his authority from the first beast (13:12), but he uses it to force people to worship the dragon. Jesus derives his authority from God, but he uses it to call humans to worship God. (Incidentally, the fact that the second beast gets its authority from the first beast is one of the reasons for believing that the second beast symbolizes the local representatives of the Roman Empire. They were the ones who carried out the persecution, but their power to do it came from Rome.) The second beast performs his miracles to deceive the people (13:14), but Jesus performs his to reveal God to the people.

The second beast, like the first, has incredible power. He commands the people to make an image of the first beast, and then he gives breath to the image (13:15). This may refer to the fact that images of Caesar had been erected in a number of cities, and they made Caesar seem real and present. Or it may refer to the fact that the second beast represents the local officials of the empire, and it is they who actually bring Caesar to life for the people. Either way, they caused "those who would not worship the image of the beast to be killed" (13:15).

The second beast, like the first, lives in every time and place. In empires other than Rome, people have been pressed to worship false gods. From seas other than the Mediterranean, spiritual monsters have arisen. In regions other than Asia Minor and in centuries other than the first, Christians have been persecuted and martyred for the sake of the faith. Rome is certainly the first false kingdom suggested by the two beasts, but it is not the only one. Caesar is certainly the first false god suggested by Revelation, but he is not the only one. The pattern continues throughout history, and no one should be surprised. The power, after all, comes from the dragon, and, as Revelation teaches us, he still roams the earth.

The final image in chapter 13 is perhaps the best known in the entire book of Revelation: the mark of the beast. The second beast marks its followers by emblazoning the number "666" on their right hands or foreheads. The mark matters: "No one can buy or sell who does not have the mark" (13:16b-17a). The beast controls all commerce; only his followers can prosper.

The number of the beast is a subject of great discussion. In both Greek and Hebrew, it was common to equate numbers with names. This practice even had a name, "gematria." Gematria was frequently used in apocalypses of the first century, and Revelation is not an exception. The device worked by equating the letters of the alphabet (whether Hebrew or Greek) with numbers. If you added the numerical values of the letters in a person's name, the total was considered that person's number. John says the number of the beast is 666. But what does this number mean? John says you can figure it out if you think about it (13:18b).

That seems like a strange claim for a number that scholars are still arguing about two thousand years later. Furthermore, anyone can convert letters to numbers, add them up, and come up with a total, but when you start with the total, 666 for instance, that number can be the sum of the letters in any number of names. "This calls for wisdom," John adds in Revelation 13:18a, and indeed it does. As mentioned above, over the course of history the beast has been identified with many different world leaders. The number of the beast has remained a mystery until the present day.

The most likely solution to the problem is that 666 refers to the first-century emperor Nero. New Testament scholar Bruce Metzger puts it as clearly as anyone: "If we add the numerical values in the Hebrew spelling of the name Neron Caesar we obtain 666; on the other hand, since his name can equally well be spelled without the last N, if we omit the final N, the total will be 616" (Metzger, 76–77). Interestingly, some ancient copies of the Scripture say the number is 666 while others say it is 616. Metzger claims that Nero is the only name that satisfies both.

Sometimes 666 has been thought to be a code intended to keep Roman officials from figuring out that the beast was the local face of the Roman Empire. This is unlikely since the Romans were just as familiar with gematria as the early Christians. They had all the information they needed to break the "code." Far more likely, the number was used for one or both of these reasons: (1) The number 666 signified the imperfection of the beast, in contrast to 777, which signified perfection. (2) The lack of a specific answer to the identity of the one bearing the mark 666 may actually be its meaning. That is, the identity of 666 may be left deliberately vague because the beast is not any one historical figure at all. Instead, the beast is present in various figures in every age, and will certainly be present in full force in the final crescendo of evil in the last days.

The purpose of chapter 13 is similar to that of chapter 12. Chapter 13 explains that even though Christ has already won the ultimate victory on the cross and has already won the heavenly battle against the evil kingdom, Satan has not yet been cast from the earth. Christians live in an interim time in which they still suffer, but even during this time they have been given enough hope to carry them through all the tribulation that remains. Victory, says God in this chapter, is on the way, and that is enough (13:10).

Blessed Assurance (Rev 14)

To this message of assurance, John adds three visions in chapter 14 that underscore his point. The three visions are (1) the Lamb and the 144,000, (2) the messages of the three angels, and (3) the reaping of the harvest on earth. The unholy trinity has had its say. Now the Triune God will have his.

In the first vision, John sees the Lamb standing on Mount Zion, that enduring symbol of the presence of God at the heart of the Jewish nation. With him are the 144,000. We encountered them in chapter 7 where they represented the totality of the redeemed, just as they do here. Chapter 14 adds an important detail: "It is these who have not defiled themselves with women, for they are virgins; these follow the Lamb wherever he goes. They have been redeemed from humankind as first fruits for God and the Lamb" (14:4).

Most likely, this does not mean that the 144,000 are literal virgins. The Old Testament often uses the terms "fornication" or "adultery," and a similar idea is implied here. The physical unfaithfulness of Hosea's wife Gomer, for instance, is clearly an image for the spiritual unfaithfulness of the nation Israel (Metzger, 78). In much the same fashion, Revelation often uses images of sexual fidelity to refer to the faithfulness or unfaithfulness of his followers.

Here the term "virgins" refers to those who had refused to worship Caesar and remained faithful to God.

The number 144,000 indicates the completeness of the redeemed, just as it did in chapter 7. All have the name of the Lamb written on their foreheads (14:1), and all join in singing praises to God. This is the church universal in its entirety, and all of them have both the mark and the song of the Spirit. They sing a new song that only they can learn. How else could it be? The redeemed have new lives to sing about and new hearts from which to sing. Only they could possibly learn this song. They make a magnificent picture. No matter what transpires in the fallen world around us, the church endures, singing on Mount Zion at the side of the Lamb.

In the second vision of chapter 14, John sees three angels. The first proclaims the gospel and calls people to faith in God (14:6-7). A second tells of the fall of Babylon (14:8). (John will tell us more about this in chapter 19.) A third angel announces that those who have the mark of the beast on them will "drink the wine of God's wrath" (14:9-11). This vision assures believers that the persecutors of the church will ultimately be conquered.

In the final vision of this chapter, John witnesses the reaping of the harvest that has been sown on the earth (14:14-20). An angel comes out of the temple in heaven and calls to "one like the Son of Man, sitting on a cloud with a golden crown on his head" (14:14) and tells this angel to swing his sharp sickle and reap the harvest. With one mighty swing, he reaps the entire harvest of the whole earth. Then another angel comes from the temple in heaven bearing a sharp sickle. An angel from the altar of heaven tells this angel to swing his sickle and gather the grapes from the vineyards of the earth. He does, and the grapes are thrown into the "great wine press of the wrath of God" (14:19). When the wine press is trodden, what flows is not wine but blood "as high as a horse's bridle for a distance of about two hundred miles" (14:20).

The point of this vision is clear. The wine press of God's wrath will one day crush those who have chosen to be his enemies and worshiped false gods. His victory will be so total that the blood will flow as high as a horse's bridle. This frightening phrase is figurative language, to be sure, but that does not diminish the fact that it depicts a God who appears merciless to some. In order to understand this, one key is to remember how tenacious Satan has been in his attack on God's kingdom. God has exhausted all other measures, but the evil one still stalks God's people and inflicts grievous wounds upon them. He would still annihilate them if he could. Therefore, the only way God can deliver his children to ultimate peace is to destroy evil totally.

Another key to understanding this picture of a seemingly merciless God is to read this passage as though we were first-century Christians. Twenty centuries make a difference in how such things are perceived. Two thousand years ago, twenty-first-century sensitivities did not apply. Christians were being persecuted and killed. The total defeat of their persecutors was to them welcome news. Some would say that Revelation reflects an idea of God that was shaped by the time-bound perspective of the first century. Their idea would be that God has now revealed more of himself to us so that we know he is more merciful than this apocalyptic picture of him reveals. Frankly, I think this idea has some merit, but I would suggest on the other hand that our own time-bound perspective may be blinding us to the reality of the wrath of God. That the Bible never backs away from wrath should give us pause. The enemies of God and his people, John says, will be totally destroyed, never to rise and inflict their evil again. In the kingdom of God, this is good news.

At the beginning of this chapter, we noted that Revelation 12–14 speak to the question, "Why must we suffer so grievously?" What it says is this: We suffer because the battle is not over, and because the father of lies still has power on the earth "for a little while." But he has already been defeated in the eternal realm of heaven, and his final end on this earth is near.

Nevertheless, the end is not yet. The terrifying imagery with which chapter 14 ends is about to be intensified. In the next section of Revelation, the seven bowls of God's wrath will be poured out on "those who had the mark of the beast, and who worshiped its image" (16:2). The contents of those bowls will set our teeth on edge.

1. What is the meaning of the dragon?

_____

_____

_____

_____

_____

2. Why do you think chapters 12–14 stand between the seven trumpets and the seven bowls?

_____

_____

_____

_____

_____

3. What message do chapters 12–14 offer to the church?

_____

_____

_____

_____

_____

4. For what did the first beast stand? What other interpretations have been given across the years?

_____

_____

_____

_____

_____

5. For what does the second beast stand?

_____

_____

_____

_____

_____

6. What is the meaning of the number 666? Whose number is it?

_____

_____

_____

_____

_____

7. If you were naming the greatest enemy of the church today, what would it be?

_____

_____

_____

_____

_____

8. Where are Christians being persecuted in the world today?

_____

_____

_____

_____

_____

The Seven Bowls

Now John moves to the last of the three cycles of judgment, the seven bowls of God's wrath. As chapter 15 opens, seven angels are preparing to pour the contents of their seven bowls on the earth. John calls these bowls portents or signs. That is, they are symbols of a higher reality rather than literal bowls.

The judgments that will pour from the seven bowls are the most severe we have encountered, but John tells us that they also are the last (15:1). The word "last" might be puzzling since we have already seen that the three sets of judgments overlap considerably and cannot be a chronological description of what is to happen. One example of this overlap is that each of the bowls corresponds precisely to each of the seven trumpets. The first trumpet and the bowl unleash judgments that fall on the earth, the second on the sea, the third on the rivers and fountains, and the fourth on the sun. The fifth involves darkness, the sixth the Euphrates River, and the seventh a loud voice that precipitates lightning, thunder, and an earthquake. In spite of this obvious overlap, however, the bowls nevertheless intimate a chronological end of judgment.

Like the seals and the trumpets, the bowls have a particular purpose in Revelation. While the seals revealed the mystery of God's purposes contained in the great scroll, and the trumpets announced God's victory over the evil that now attacked the church, the bowls hold out a promise that God's judgment on the wicked will one day reach an end. All the cycles call people to repentance. All of them tell of the coming judgment. But the bowls, as terrible as their judgments are, promise that one day God's judgment will come to an end.

Likely, as you read these two chapters in Revelation, you will ask some deep questions. Some of them will be the same questions you had as you read the passages pertaining to the seals and the trumpets. Why are these judgments so harsh? How could God be justified in inflicting them? What could possibly be their purpose? Job asked these same questions during his tribulations, and countless human beings have asked them since. The limitations of human understanding engulf us so that we are only able to "see through a glass darkly" (1 Cor 13:12), but if we do not begin to address these questions, the modern world will miss the message of Revelation.

A good starting place for our brief reflection might be verse 1, which says that with the bowls "the wrath of God is ended." Does this phrase mean that God has thoroughly vented his anger and is now emotionally spent? Or does it mean that God has gotten even with the forces of evil and is now finished delivering retribution? Both explanations are obviously lacking. The idea that God has now vented his anger to the point of satisfaction makes God into a temperamental little person who cares about nothing so much as his own gratification. The other idea, that God has now seen to it that Satan and his followers get what is coming to them, makes God into a revenge-seeker, a kind of divine Dirty Harry. Surely, Revelation means something more than this when it says that "the wrath of God is ended."

A better explanation is based on the nature of the book of Revelation. Revelation is about God's struggle against evil, against Satan and against Satan's servants, and it grandly announces that the end of the story is God's total victory over evil. When Revelation 15:1 says the wrath of God is ended, it means that total victory is finally accomplished. There is no more need for the wrath of God. It has done its work. The enemy is now vanquished forever.

His wrath, the passage claims, is just. In our culture we tend to see only the negative and destructive side of anger. For us, anger has caused too much pain, too much suffering, and too much grief. We forget that anger is not only a tool that destroys the good; it can also be a tool that destroys evil. If we were angry enough about starvation, we could stop it. If we were angry enough about torture, we could end it. If we were angry enough about corruption, we could corral it. If we were angry enough about greed, we could check it. The judgments of the bowls affirm that God is angry enough about evil that he will in fact destroy it.

But the God our culture exalts is a tepid God who is too kind to be angry at people, too mild to run out any moneychangers, too democratic to rage against corruption, too modern to make people feel guilty about their sin. Simply put, our culture regards it as unthinkable that God could be angry, though it is of course permissible for us. But we can be sure of this: When God gives the church to the world, and the powers of the world persecute it, he is angry. When God puts enough food on the earth to feed everyone and yet people starve, he is angry. When God creates the earth for the good of human beings and human beings pollute it for profit, he is angry. When God gives us wonderful bodies to enjoy and we abuse them with drugs and drink and food and over-work, he is angry. When God gives us amazing abilities and we use them for nothing more than to accumulate wealth for ourselves, he is angry. When God gives us the gospel and we rip churches and individuals apart with our divisive spirits, God is angry. John sees all this, and he thunders a terrible and wonderful assurance: one day God will finally prevail over Satan, and with his anger will wipe creation clean of all the poison stains of evil.

Scholars call this promise "eschatological." That is, it is not just a promise that Rome will end. It is a promise that the world as we know it, the world corrupted by wrong, will end. It is a promise of a day when "Every valley shall be lifted up, and every mountain and hill be made low . . ." (Isa 40:4). It is a promise and message of hope for the church of the ages. The struggle against sin, evil, and suffering will one day be finished forever. There will be no more starving children, no more broken hearts, no more cruel wars, no more stinging lies, no more lethal illnesses, no more callous hearts, no more empty chasing of the wind, no more anguished souls. In fact, there will be no more death, no more tears, no more pain (Rev 21:4), for evil will have met its end, and we shall say with John that the wrath of God is finished and his enemy is no more. The vision of the bowls, which we have so often regarded as terrifying, is intended to share this reassurance with both struggling churches and disheartened saints.

The Two Visions of Revelation 15

Chapter 15 contains two visions, although they might well be viewed as two parts of the same vision. First is the vision of the saints standing beside the sea singing of victory, and the second is a vision of the seven angels as they are given the bowls. The saints are seen as victors, as those who have conquered. We might expect the text to say that the Lamb had conquered, but it specifically says *they* had conquered, meaning the saints. Could this be? Could mere human beings have actually conquered the cosmic forces of evil? After all, the power of Satan is described as both superhuman and devastating. The answer is yes. These conquerors have succeeded because they are part of the forces of God. They are co-laborers with him (1 Cor 3:9; 2 Cor 6:1), and they have received power, as Acts 1:8 said, after the Holy Ghost has come upon them. This is clearly the power that enabled them to endure.

Endurance is no small matter for Christians. John extols this virtue, and so did Jesus: "But the one who endures to the end will be saved" (Matt 24:13). The first time this part of John's letter to the seven churches was read in one of those congregations, it must have electrified the worshipers. Their thoughts would have been, "Yes, there is hope beyond our present struggles. Yes, we shall one day stand with all the saints by the heavenly sea and celebrate the great victory. John has seen it!" This is a vision that empowered the church in a time of tribulation, and it is a vision that can empower the church of today.

But John is not content to say that these believers endured. In fact, he does not say it. Their endurance is simply obvious in the fact that the saints are there. The text says they conquered. Their endurance itself was a power that conquered. The Indian nation learned this under Gandhi. The American Civil Rights marchers learned it under King. The Jews who endured the savagery of Hitler's gas chambers learned it from their ancient faith.

By their endurance of tribulation, and by the power of the Lamb that was slain, the saints conquered (Rev 15:2) the beast and its image, conquered Rome and its phony god Caesar, and con-quered all the beastly kingdoms of history that fall under the sway of the dragon. Christians do not suffer for nothing. We are warriors in a cosmic battle. Every time we right a wrong, every time we defend the weak, every time we feed the hungry, every time we heal the hurting, every time we free the oppressed, every time we sup-press greed, every time we defy racism, every time we love the loveless, every time we speak for righteousness in the public arena, every time we proclaim forgiveness by the power of Jesus Christ, we are partners with God in the decimation of the power of evil. Those who stand by the glassy sea are God's partners, and so they are con-querors indeed.

The heavenly sea by which the conquerors stand is the same one we saw in Revelation 4, but this time the sea looks like "glass mixed with fire" (15:2). The fire is God's judgment, and it is mingled into the sea, which is the symbolic boundary of heaven. God's wrath is part of what separates the new Jerusalem from the old one. The conquerors stand safely on the other side of God's wrath, sealed in the kingdom by the judgments it wrought.

With so much to celebrate, they hold "harps of God" (15:2) in their hands and sing the song of Moses and of the Lamb. The song of Moses, of course, is a song of deliverance. The song of Moses was a song Moses recited, recorded in Deuteronomy 32, just before he died. The song here is not the same song that Moses sang, but it is like Moses' song in that it is a song of deliverance, a celebration that God has delivered his people from slavery in Egypt to the promised land. The song of the Lamb, of course, is the song of the new Israel, also a song of deliverance, this time the deliverance that has been secured by the conquerors through the power of the Lamb that was slain.

In the second vision of chapter 15, John sees the seven angels who will deliver the final judgments. As we have already discussed, many of us question the justice of these judgments, but Revelation has anticipated our objection. In three different ways, John indicates that these judgments are justified. First, John reports that the angels come with their judgments out of the "temple of the tent of witness" (15:5). This temple strongly resembles the wilderness tabernacle of Moses' time, but it is not Moses' tabernacle; it is rather the heavenly model of which the earthly tabernacle was a pale imitation. The fact that it was a "tent of witness" meant that it spoke to the people of the presence of God. In other words, the seven bowls of God's wrath come from God's most inner sanctum, and so they are justified by their source.

Second, John underscores the holiness of the judgments again when one of the four living creatures places the bowls in the hands of the angels. The four living creatures, you recall, had summoned the four horsemen of the apocalypse. They are likely angelic beings of the highest order. Their clothing resembles that of the risen Christ (1:13) and so emphasizes their holiness. The judgments are sanctified once again because they are passed from the inner sanctum of God by holy angel to holy angel.

The third declaration of the justice of the judgments is perhaps the most striking. Verse 8 says that the temple was filled with smoke from the power and glory of the Lord, and that no one could enter it until the plagues were ended. Why could no one enter? Very simply, God was in the temple in the full splendor of his glory and in the full majesty of his power. After all, he was engaged with Satan in a battle to the death. If no person could see him and live in the time of Moses (Exod 33:20), how could anyone possibly behold him in his full glory as he is about to win the final victory? Here, if anywhere, the glory of God is too radiant for human eyes. Here, if anywhere, the power of God is too great for human comprehension. And here, if anywhere, the wrath of God is too terrible for human imaginings. In other words, the judgments of God are justified because they come from God. They come from a glory too great for us now to experience in full. (This is much like the answer Job received when God was asked to justify his ways to Job: "Where were you when I laid the foundation of the earth? Tell me, if you have understanding" [Job 38:4].) John himself is content to trust the justice of these judgments, having seen just an intimation of the power and the glory of "the one who lives forever and ever" (15:7). His implication is clear: after the seven plagues are ended, after justice is established, after sin is defeated, we shall be able to enter the temple of the tent of witness (15:8), and we shall at last see him face to face.

The Bowls of Wrath (Rev 16)

Just as it was with the seals and the trumpets, the first four bowls and the last three form separate groups. The first four bowls release plagues that affect the natural order, while the last three release plagues that affect the political order. We will consider the four natural plagues first.

When the first bowl is poured out on the earth, those who bear the mark of the beast now bear a "foul and painful sore" (15:2). When the second bowl is poured out on the sea, its waters become "like the blood of a corpse" (15:3), that is, like the blood of the martyrs who had died for the faith. When the third bowl is poured out on the rivers and streams and makes their water "like blood" (15:4) as well, no one on earth could turn a blind eye to the cruel and unjust executions of the martyrs. (Verse 6 states explicitly that this is what the blood symbolizes.) The fourth bowl is the only one not taken from the plagues on Egypt. When the horrors of the fourth bowl are poured out on the sun, its searing blaze is allowed to scorch God's enemies.

Notice that God is not destroying the natural elements on which his wrath is poured. Rather, he is using nature to exercise his judgment on those who have chosen to follow the beast (Caird, 202). He uses sores to afflict them; he uses the absence of water, now become blood, to parch them; and he uses the heat of the sun to scorch them. This is not God's judgment on nature; it is God's judgment on evil people who persecute the church.

God had sent natural plagues before. When Pharaoh refused to listen to Moses' pleas for the freedom of his people, God released similar plagues on Egypt. Six of the bowl plagues, as a matter of fact, three of the natural plagues and three of the political ones, are exact parallels to the Egyptian plagues. The only exception is the fourth. The clear lesson is not the specific nature of the plagues. It is that God will now use the power he once used against Pharaoh to thwart the beast and all his evil kingdoms.

An important parenthesis follows the account of the third bowl. In it, the "angel of the waters" offers this affirmation: "You are just, O Holy One, who are and were, for you have judged these things; because they shed the blood of saints and prophets, you have given them blood to drink. It is what they deserve" (16:4-5)! In verse 7, the altar itself responds with a loud amen: "Yes, O Lord God, the Almighty, your judgments are true and just!" This is the same affirmation that was made in the song of Moses and the Lamb in chapter 15, but here the claim is made more specific. Not only is God himself just; God's actions against the persecutors of the church are just.

The repetition of this affirmation tells us that John thinks it is important for his readers to understand this. It suggests that John anticipates the question that so many have asked over the centuries: Do these seemingly terrible actions make into God a vengeful God? Some have claimed that John was vengeful and that he simply ascribed his own judgments to God. Others have claimed that the suffering church was vengeful and that John then projected their vengeful spirits onto God. These are the explanations of cynicism, but there are other explanations. The best in my view is the explanation of faith. This explanation says that the pouring out of the bowls of wrath is a symbol that God has taken up the cause of his people. The enemies of his people are now his enemies. They need no longer fear the Roman beast because God, not Caesar, is Lord. Neither need they fear any other beast, because God will destroy all powers that deal cruelly with his children.

All the depictions of this destruction given in the three cycles of plagues are intended to call people to repentance, but the persecutors of God's people, the followers of the beast, still curse God and do not repent (16:9). Even after these greatest of natural catastrophes, their hearts are hardened just as Pharaoh's was. The recalcitrance of the human heart is ever with us.

From the fifth, sixth, and seventh bowls, judgment falls on Rome, the political agent of the sufferings of the church. Rome typically extended a great deal of tolerance toward the religions of its conquered nations, but unlike the others, Christianity was not minding its own business. It was spreading like wildfire through the empire, encouraging Roman subjects to deny the divinity of Caesar and to follow another God. It was nothing but trouble. As a result, some Roman leaders felt that they could not ignore this threat, and they mobilized the power of Rome to attempt to extinguish the fledgling first-century church.

John reminds the Christians that the Romans are no match for God. When the judgment of the fifth bowl fell, it fell on "the throne of the beast, and its kingdom was plunged into darkness" (16:10). Once again, echoes of the Old Testament are heard here, for the fifth bowl parallels the plague of darkness that fell on Egypt. The beast, we remember, is at the first level Rome, the intellectual, economic, and political light of the ancient world. With these judgments, that light is plunged into darkness. The light that was Rome—not the Christian church—was extinguished.

The sixth bowl is poured out, and its contents dry up the waters of the river Euphrates completely. With the river no longer there to serve as a natural barrier, the great beast Rome is now left with no way to hold back the eastern forces that have tried to destroy it for so long. The Euphrates had never dried up before, but then again neither had the Red Sea when Moses led the Israelites across it. This is no mere natural event; this is God at work. Rome is about to fall, and so is the kingdom of evil of which Rome is a part.

First, however, the final battle must be engaged. Three demonic spirits "like frogs" (associated in the first century with sinister forces) come forth, one each from the mouths of the dragon, the beast, and the false prophet (or the second beast). These demonic spirits "go abroad to the kings of the whole world, to assemble them for battle, on the great day of God the Almighty" (16:14). They are called together to make battle against Rome, but we must remember that Rome is but a single manifestation of the beast. Rome is obviously intended, but it is simply not credible to interpret this passage as referring only to Rome. The battle being prepared is a cosmic fight against Satan himself. This is the final showdown between God and the kingdom of darkness.

John says that the evil spirits assemble the kings of the whole world for battle at a place called Armageddon. This, of course, is one of the most famous passages in Revelation. Questions about it abound. When will the battle of Armageddon take place? Where will it occur? Why will it occur? Is it simply a physical battle to be fought at a specific earthly location, or is it a spiritual battle that takes place in a realm beyond the physical? Answers can be difficult because, contrary to popular belief, relatively little is said about Armageddon in the Bible. In fact, the word "Armageddon" itself is the source of a great deal of confusion.

The word as it occurs in the text is "Harmagedon," a Greek transliteration of the Hebrew "Har-Megiddo," or "the mountain of Megiddo" (Beasley-Murray, 245). Unfortunately for those who want to identify the physical location of the battle, however, there is no mountain of Megiddo. There is a town called Megiddo located in the plain of Esdraelon (also called the Jezreel Valley) in Israel, but it has no mountain. Nevertheless, many Bible students have concluded that this plain is the site of the battle that will occur at the end of history. Any effort to locate the battle of Armageddon, however, will ultimately come up empty.

This is because Armageddon is not to be a literal historical battle. Revelation is about God's final victory over Satan and his forces, and they are a far greater enemy that any on earth. Would it make sense for Revelation to near its conclusion on a battlefield where only earthly powers are defeated? This battle appears to be the climax of the entire book. It is more than a clash of arms on an earthly battlefield. It is a war to the last between forces larger than history and larger than us. Once again, Paul gave us a clue: "For our struggle is not against enemies of blood and flesh, but against the rulers, against the authorities, against the cosmic powers of this present darkness, against the spiritual forces of evil in the heavenly places" (Eph 6:12). In my view, it does not matter if we have difficulty deciphering the word "Harmagedon," for this is not the name of a place at all; it is the name of an event (Beasley-Murray, 246), and a spiritual one at that. Armageddon is not the final battle on earth. It is the final battle in God's eternal universe.

This idea that Armageddon is to be a literal battle in Israel leads some Christians to unwarranted political conclusions. The thinking goes like this: The Jews must occupy Israel in order for the battle of Armageddon to occur there. If the battle of Armageddon does not occur, the second coming of Christ cannot occur. Therefore, Israel must occupy the land on which it sits, or God will not be able to accomplish his purposes. And it then follows that Israel must be supported in any action it takes. No other point of view can be allowed.

Of course, this kind of thinking is a danger to peace in the Middle East, but it is also a danger to faith. It teaches that God's plan to conquer Satan can be thwarted by earthly politics. But this contradicts a central point that Revelation makes, namely, that God is Lord over all kingdoms; he is not subject to them. This viewpoint also means that God is locked in by the past and must therefore condone wrong if Israel happens to be the perpetrator. As absurd as this may sound, many sincere Christians adhere to this position even though is based on an erroneous understanding of the Bible. There are many good reasons to give the modern state of Israel our support, but the teaching of the Scripture about Armageddon is not one of them.

The larger truth at the core of Revelation is that God will prevail in the battle against Babylon and its lord, and earthly kingdoms, so often corrupted by the devil, shall all become "the kingdom of our Lord and of his Messiah, and he will reign forever and ever" (11:15). As the account of the sixth bowl ends, the forces are assembled. All is in readiness. The great battle is about to begin.

At last, the contents of the seventh bowl are poured out into the air, and amid thunder, lightning, and the greatest earthquake imaginable, the great Babylon is destroyed. Then God says with a loud voice, "It is done!" On the cross Jesus had said, "It is finished" (John 19:30). It was not only his earthly life that was finished; it was his work of atonement. These similar words in Revelation tell us that the wrath of God is at an end, that the plagues of God's judgments are over. The destruction of Babylon is about to be described, but the end is already set. When judgment falls on Babylon, the end of suffering, the end of evil, the end of injustice will have come.

The meaning of the bowls is not obscure. The bowls are first, like the other judgments, a call to repentance, and then they are a dramatic statement that the wrath of God will come to an end. When the bowls are finally empty, God's wrath is spent. The destruction of Babylon is assured. Deliverance is at hand. Christians of every age who writhe under the persecutions of the dragon are finally vindicated. The day of the Lord is near.

1. Is God's judgment at work in the world today? Where do you see it happening?

_____

_____

_____

_____

_____

2. What does Revelation mean when it says that God's judgments are just? How could they be just when they are so terrible?

_____

_____

_____

_____

_____

3. Is God's vengeance different than that of human beings?

_____

_____

_____

_____

_____

4. What do the bowls mean? What facet of truth do they show that the plagues of the seals and the trumpets do not?

_____

_____

_____

_____

_____

5. What and where do you think the battle of Armageddon will be?

_____

_____

_____

_____

_____

6. Why do you think the battle of Armageddon is necessary?

_____

_____

_____

_____

_____

At the end of Revelation 16, the seventh bowl is poured into the air, but it takes all of chapters 17 and 18 for John to describe the result. What follows the emptying of this bowl is the fall of Babylon itself.

The place to start in understanding this section of the Apocalypse is to ask what John means by "Babylon." Babylon was of course a historical city and empire that conquered much of the ancient Near East, eventually including Israel. But this had occurred six hundred years before Revelation was written. Certainly John did not mean the literal Babylon.

Babylon had come to mean much more to the Israelites. When the Babylonian Empire conquered Judah, they took much of its population away to live in exile in Babylon. After seventy years of wondering how they could sing the Lord's song in a strange land, the Israelites were suddenly released. Their memories of those years in Babylon never mention Hanging Gardens and Hammurabi's Code, but they do mention the strangeness and suffering they experienced in this land where they lived for so long. To many of them, the exile seemed like an endless time of homelessness. (Some adapted, prospered, and chose to stay there.) Their exile ended when the Persians defeated the Babylonians and Cyrus the Persian ruler released them. Many made the long journey home, but their memories were so terrible that the very name "Babylon" came to represent the kingdom of evil on the earth. This is why it was natural for early Christians to think of Rome as their Babylon. As we shall see, however, they also realized that Babylon represented far more than Rome.

Babylon for the Israelites came to mean hubris and greed, vanity and self-absorption, hostility and inhumanity. As used in

Revelation, it is the fallen quality of human culture, the madness of worldly power, the cruelty of corrupted wealth, and the misuse of vainglorious learning. Babylon is the quintessential city of evil, the model city of Satan. It is the antithesis of the kingdom of God. It is the seat of the Babylonian Empire and it is first-century Rome, but it is also New York and Paris and London. It is Sao Paulo and Mexico City and Shanghai. It is Washington and Moscow and Beijing. It is Atlanta and Nashville and Dallas. It is Tampa and Miami and Los Angeles. Babylon is the sum of all evil and the totality of all opposition to God. It is the false community that dominates the earth in every time, pursuing its own ends, indulging its own excesses, and worshiping its own gods.

The two chapters in Revelation that relate to the fall of Babylon are nestled between John's three cycles of judgments and the coming of the glory of God. Their placement is no accident. The cycles of judgment culminate in the destruction of Babylon, the sum of all evil. Only when they are over is the stage finally cleared for what comes next: the return of Christ in glory.

Of course, John is writing not only of the collapse of a single city but also of the collapse of "this present darkness" (Eph 6:12), of all the evil reality human beings know. John is writing of the end of all things dark and dangerous, all things that inflict pain and suffering upon God's children, all things that lure women and men away from the ways of God. That is why these terrible chapters of destruction are such fantastically good news. Let us look at each chapter in succession. Chapter 17 tells of the coming the fall of Babylon in highly symbolic language. Chapter 18 laments the fallen city. The destruction itself is never described.

The Fall of Babylon (Rev 17)

The imagery of chapter 17 is complex, so it might help to summarize the chapter briefly. Then we will be better able to try to understand what it means. In the first part of the chapter, John describes the vision he saw, and in the second part he records an angel's explanation of this vision.

In the first verse, one of the bowl angels invites John to see a vision of a prostitute sitting on "many waters." The angel then carries John away "in the spirit into a wilderness" (v. 3), where he sees the prostitute sitting on a scarlet beast. The beast is hideous. On it are written blasphemous names. It has seven heads and ten horns, making it clear that this is the same beast as the one that came from the sea in chapter 13. At first glance, the woman likely appears beautiful, clothed in opulent finery and holding a golden cup. But John sees that she is not beautiful after all. Her dazzling golden cup holds only her phony idols and the impurities of her intercourse with the kings. On her forehead is written her ugly name: "Babylon the great, mother of whores and of the earth's abominations" (v. 5). Finally, John sees that the prostitute is inebriated, having drunk deeply of the blood of the Christ followers.

This vision confounds and amazes John, but the angel promises to help him understand. He does offer an explanation, but he also speaks in a puzzling riddle: "The beast that you saw was, and is not, and is about to ascend from the bottomless pit and go to destruction" (v. 8). All the redeemed, the angel says, will be amazed by this. In fact, you are most likely amazed yourself. After all, a beast that was, and is not, and is about to appear again is a pretty amazing thing.

Then the angel says that the seven heads are seven mountains on which the woman is seated, and they are also seven kings (notice that the symbol has more than one meaning). There is an eighth king as well, the angel says, and that king is the beast. "This calls for a mind that has wisdom" (v. 9), says the angel, in what may be the understatement of the entire book. In addition, the ten horns are kings as well, but these are kings who have not yet received their kingdoms. When they do, they will yield their authority to the beast and reign with him, but only for an hour. Under the leadership of the beast, they will make war on the Lamb, but in the end the Lamb will utterly defeat them. He, after all, is the King of kings and the Lord of lords. He will emerge from the battle victorious, and when he does his followers will stand with him in victory.

The angel says that there is also a second symbol for all the nations of the earth, and that is the waters where the whore is seated. This symbolism is easy to understand because it was by these waters that Babylon had commerce with the other nations. Finally, however, these nations who profited from supplying Babylon with luxuries, the nations who were the lackeys of Babylon, will turn on the whore with whom they have fornicated and destroy her. In other words, God is so great that he is able to use the beast and his followers as instruments with which to destroy evil. At the end of the explanation, the angel reminds John that the woman is "the great city that rules over the kings of the earth" (v. 18). Now that we have summarized the passage, let us think about what this bizarre picture could possibly mean.

Once the obscure imagery is unraveled, the meaning of the chapter will become clear. Modern readers need a considerable amount of help with the unraveling. These symbols are two thousand years old; they are couched in the strange and unfamiliar language of apocalyptic literature; and they are often drawn from some of the most obscure portions of the Old Testament. In other words, they were written in a first-century frame of reference that is vastly different from ours, and they therefore require some effort to understand. The effort is worth it.

First of all, let's examine the vision itself. The prostitute (the NRSV refers to her by the cruder name "whore") is Babylon. Verse 5 tells us this plainly, saying that her name is written on her forehead. This is her name: "Babylon the great, mother of whores and of earth's abomination." The lurid image of a whore is used because Babylon (or Rome, or the kingdom of evil, as we have already seen) has wantonly betrayed the living God and given herself to other gods. This use of the word "whore" (or "harlot," "prostitute") is consistent with the way it is used in numerous Old Testament passages. It is a word used to describe the repulsive faithlessness of the people of God. It has nothing to do with sexual immorality.

When one of the beasts of chapter 13 reappears here in chapter 17, he is marked once again by his seven heads and ten horns. This beast, like so many of John's symbols, has multiple meanings. He represents Rome in both chapters, to be sure, but in chapter 13 he is the creation of Satan, while in chapter 17 he *is* Satan. He is even colored red, just as Satan took the form of a red dragon in chapter 12.

The meaning becomes a bit clearer when we notice that the whore is sitting on the beast. The whore is Babylon. The beast is Satan upon whom Babylon sits. The prince of darkness, in other words, is the dark reality that underlies all earthly evil. That the harlot sits on the beast says that the kingdom of evil on earth is simply the material manifestation of Satan's cosmic kingdom. This is the meaning of Babylon. When Babylon falls in the final battle, it is not some merely earthly city that falls. Satan and the whole of his evil empire will be brought to nothing.

Babylon, in fact, must be destroyed because she has been the gate through which Satan's corruption has taken over the earth. She is seated on "many waters," allowing her to spread her wanton lusts, her cruel violence, and her misshapen values to the rest of the earth. Interestingly, both Babylon and Rome sat "on many waters," Babylon on the Euphrates and Rome on (or very near) the Mediterranean. Their geographical locations allowed them to trade goods, ideas, behaviors, and values with the rest of the world. Babylon was corrupted by the prosperity that resulted from their trade (as chapter 18 will make clear). From the viewpoint of Revelation, Babylon's main export turned out to be corruption. The rulers of many smaller nations and cities had become dependent on Babylon for their own prosperity, and so they were also susceptible to the corruption that plagued Babylon. John likens this interaction to harlotry. For the sake of wealth, both the old and the new Babylon sell their souls and become heady with their own power. Therefore, the angel describes Babylon as a city with whom "the kings of the earth have committed fornication, and with the wine of whose fornication the inhabitants of the earth have become drunk" (v. 2).

Sadly, many interpreters seek to identify Babylon with a specific city and end up missing the obvious: this Scripture applies to us. Babylon was the leading culture of the world known to the biblical writers in the sixth century BC. Rome played the same role in the first century AD. Who plays such a role in the world today? Quite clearly, America does. Like the ancient empires of Babylon and Rome, America "sits on many waters," exploring many good things to the world: our inventions, our freedoms, our cultural achievements; but we should never forget that we also export our corruption, our violence, our wantonness, our godlessness, and our greed. Revelation 17 is not only a warning to Rome. It is a warning to us. This chapter of the Apocalypse is a stern reminder indeed that all nations and cultures that sit upon many waters will be called to account.

Babylon is called to account for her fornication with the kings of the earth, but she is also called to account for becoming drunk on the blood of the saints. Christian believers threatened first-century Rome. They served a God higher than Caesar, and they were vigorous about making converts. In response, Rome shed their blood. She shed so much of it, in fact, that she was not only guilty of their blood but was also drunk on it. She was giddy with the pleasure of persecuting the church, and John conveyed a promise from God to the suffering: Rome would be called to account. The new Babylon would fall.

The angel not only offers an explanation of the harlot; he also offers an explanation of the beast. The beast is a more complex image than the harlot, perhaps because the beast represents Satan and the harlot represents his simpler human pawns. Three key elements are involved in the angel's explanation of the beast.

First, the angel says, "The beast that you saw was, and is not, and is about to descend from the bottomless pit and go to destruction" (v. 8). This is a puzzling phrase. The angel repeats it in verse 9 where he says that the beast "was and is not and is to come." He does not clarify this phrase, but we can begin to understand it if we acknowledge that the beast is Satan (this would seem to be verified by the fact that the beast comes from the bottomless pit). Here is what I mean: this description of the beast as one who "was and is not and is to come" stands in deliberate contrast to the references in Revelation to God as "he who was and is and is to come" (see, for example, Rev 1:4, 8; 4:8; 11:17). The beast is God's opposite. If we understand nothing else about this phrase the angel used, we know from this contrast that the beast could not be more different from God.

Still, we are left to wonder what it means that the beast "is not." The answer most Bible scholars agree on is that Revelation must have been written during a remission of the Roman persecutions, and therefore the beast at that moment and in that sense "was not." That is, he was not a present reality in the way that he had been or would be.

The angel warns, however, that the beast will return. This prophecy has proven true repeatedly throughout history, and it will prove true when the great beast appears at the final battle. (An easier way for some to think about this passage, incidentally, is to interpret the beast as a symbol of persecution rather than a symbol of Satan himself.) Nevertheless, John and his readers need not fear the return of the beast because he is destined for destruction. He is evil from beginning to end, but now his end is near.

The angel also explains the meaning of the beast's seven heads and ten horns. The seven heads are seven mountains on which the woman is seated. This is obviously Rome at the first level of meaning, the city that sits on seven hills. At another level, however (as we have so often seen by now), lies another meaning. Since seven is the number of completeness or fullness in Revelation, the seven hills of Rome may represent the fullness of the evil as it is present in Babylon. This double meaning of Babylon should not surprise us.

We have seen it before. Actually, if only one reality were intended, John would probably not have needed a symbol.

The next image also represents more than one reality. The seven heads are seven kings, the angel says, five who have fallen, one who is alive, and one who is yet to come. The seven kings would appear to represent seven Caesars, but difficulties accompany any effort to name them. No matter which Caesar a scholar may begin with, the count does not work out to seven. In all likelihood, no specific kings are intended. In a more general way, the five kings who have fallen stand for the Caesars who have already ruled, the sixth is the current Caesar, and the seventh stands for the Caesars that are yet to come (v. 10). This seventh king, the angel adds, will reign only for a little while. This is an assurance that the reign of evil, in God's grand time scheme, is to be short. Some may try to use this passage to provide a timetable for predicting the end times, but this is clearly not what it means.

We need not fret too much about the identity of the seven kings, however, because there is an eighth king who is vastly more important. The eighth king is the most dangerous of them all. He, the angel says, is the one that was and is not. In other words, the eighth king is the beast. He belongs to the seven, to the kings of this world, and like them he is destined for destruction.

Now even more kings get in on the act, for the ten horns also turn out to be kings. These are not Roman kings like the seven, but they are future kings of other kingdoms. They will join forces with the beast to make war on the Lamb, explains the angel, but the Lamb will conquer them. In other words, these kings are earthly enemies of God and his church. They are not particular kings. Rather they stand for all earthly power that is allied with the beast. First-century Christians had no doubt about the nature of earthly power. Earthly rulers had too often inflicted suffering on both Israel and the church. They had too often adopted values contrary to righteousness. To these believers, the powers of this world were always suspect. They likely picked up this attitude from their Jewish forebears, who fed on Scriptures like Zechariah 4:6b where God said to Zerubbabel, "Not by might, nor by power, but by my spirit, says the LORD of hosts."

The vision shows a stark picture of the evil powers on the earth, the angel says, but the angel also offers hope. The Lamb will conquer. All the empires, all the nations, all the kings, even the beast himself and the dragon who is his lord, will fall in defeat.

Astoundingly, they will fall not before a general leading earthly legions but before a simple Lamb whose throat has been slit.

At the end of his explanation, the angel identifies the woman. She is "the great city that rules over the kings of the earth" (v. 18). The angel identifies Babylon vaguely for a reason: she is Babylon, she is Rome, and she is the entirety of the kingdom of evil in this world. Babylon is an image that does not stand in a one-to-one correlation with any city on earth. Babylon is a reality that is far larger than any one city. Symbols are like that (see Elisabeth Schüssler Fiorenza's discussion in *The Book of Revelation*, pp. 183 ff.).

Lament for the Fallen City (Rev 18)

Babylon has fallen. Armageddon is over. Revelation now shifts into a chapter-long lament over the city's fall. Listen to the pathos in the angel's cry: "Fallen, fallen is Babylon the great" (v. 2). The angel mourns because Babylon was not what it might have been. The city now lies in the ruins of its tragic end, an end that should never have been necessary. Chapter 18 contains painful laments over Babylon, and they come from both heaven and earth.

The Lament of Heaven (vv. 1-8)

A new angel appears in chapter 18, one with great authority (v. 1). Clearly, his words are to be taken lightly only at the peril of his hearers. The angel opens the doors of heaven so that his lament over Babylon may be heard on the earth.

The angel makes the whole earth "bright with his splendor" (v. 1), revealing the glory of God, of course, but also revealing the evils of Babylon. In the light of the angel, the city's attractions do not look nearly as appealing as they did in the dark.

The description of Babylon's failure is powerful: "her sins are heaped high as heaven" (v. 5). She is a dwelling place of demons, a haunt of foul spirits, foul birds, and dangerous beasts. She has led the nations of the earth into her own corrupt lifestyle. Nations envy her, imitate her, and ultimately follow her to destruction: "For all the nations have drunk of the wine of the wrath of her fornication . . ." (v. 3).

Babylon, the description helps us to recall, is the sum total of sinful human culture. Babylon's evil thwarts the proclamation of the gospel. It deafens the ears, distracts the minds, hardens the hearts, blurs the vision, and usurps the loyalties of its people. The lament of heaven is for all the Babylons of every age.

Today in the West, people are leaving churches in significant numbers, and they are becoming less receptive to the gospel. We in the churches wring our hands in response, and we try to locate the problem in our own failures. Surely they are leaving because of our failure to be interesting or relevant or hip. If we just adopt a new strategy, repackage the message for our age, or redefine the church, then perhaps our problems will be over. I have come to believe that this diagnosis is attractive to us because it reassures us that we can do something about the decline of faith in our world. Not that the church has not failed; in many respects it has. But the seven churches of Revelation had their failures too, and those are identified in Revelation 2 and 3. But unlike modern analysts, John is not content to say only that the church needs to change. He says instead that they are ministering in Babylon, and only God will be able to overcome the evil one. Before church people of today beat themselves up too badly, we need to remember that, especially in the West, we too minister in Babylon, the realm of the beast. Like those ancient Christians to whom John addressed the letter of Revelation, ". . . our struggle is not against enemies of blood and flesh . . ." (Eph 6:12). Like them also, we must learn to depend not on our devices and strategies but on God, who alone can master Babylon.

God has mastered Babylon, John says, and "another voice from heaven" (v. 4) reminds us that she has received justice, for "mighty is the Lord God who judges her" (v. 8). Again, her fall is not simply the result of the vengeance of God. She has sown the seeds of her own destruction. The voice cries out, "Render to her as she herself has rendered" (v. 6). She has lived in splendor, so she falls in torment. She has lived as though she would never know grief, so she grieves for the loss of all that she is (v. 7). She has persecuted God's children. She has indulged herself in affluence. She has lived as though there was no death, as though there was no judgment, and so she is "burned with fire" (v. 8). Sin carries its own consequences.

THE LAMENT OF THE EARTH (VV. 9-19)

After the voice from heaven has spoken, laments are heard from the earth as well. The laments come from the kings of the earth, from the merchants of the earth, and finally from the shipmasters and sailors of the earth. All of them weep because, when Babylon fell, they lost the source of their security and prosperity. Their gods had fallen, so the kings could no longer rest comfortably in bed at night. The city was bankrupt, so the merchants could no longer sell their wares. The worldwide trade that had made them rich had vanished, so the sailors and shipmasters could no longer profit. Their laments are awful groans from those who have placed their faith in a cruel and deceptive beast.

THE SINS OF BABYLON (VV. 20-24)

The last part of chapter 18 is a powerfully poetic passage and is best appreciated when read aloud. It begins with a call for heaven to rejoice, for Babylon at last has met its judge. Its evils will be perpetrated no longer, and Babylon will be no more. An angel throws a millstone into the sea and pronounces, "With such violence Babylon the great city will be thrown down, and will be found no more . . ." (v. 21).

A great multitude in heaven responds, singing, "Hallelujah!" Hallelujah, for God has at last destroyed evil. Hallelujah, for God has delivered his people. Hallelujah, for God has obliterated the dark forces that lead humans to self-destruction. Hallelujah not because Caesar got what was coming to him but because God has delivered his creation from suffering and pain, from tears and sorrow, from death and destruction.

Conclusion

And so, in Revelation, great Babylon meets its dismal end. But in the meantime, Babylon is still with us. The earth is still the realm of darkness. The battle of Armageddon has not yet been fought. Babylon is alive and continues its fight against God. We had best not fall too deeply in love with Babylon or grow too attached to its ways. This world, while it is the gift of God, has been corrupted by evil. This present order must, and surely will, meet its destruction at the hand of God.

To place our faith in any government, any economic system, any luxury, any power, any human indulgence is to place our faith in what is temporary and is fated for destruction. Revelation calls that reality Babylon, but Revelation also contains another message: when we are wrapped too tightly in the deadly arms of Babylon, we are to rejoice, for the great city is about to be destroyed by the holy fire of God.

In the vision John sees, the fall of Babylon is now complete. Dreaded Armageddon is over. The final victory is about to come.

1. What is the message of the vision of the beast and the great whore?

_____

_____

_____

_____

_____

2. What does "Babylon" mean in Revelation?

_____

_____

_____

_____

_____

3. Where do you see Babylon in the world in which you live? Is there a particular behavior that identifies it for you?

_____

_____

_____

_____

_____

4. If the world as you and I know it were gone tomorrow, what would you lament?

_____

_____

_____

_____

_____

5. Why must Babylon be defeated?

_____

_____

_____

_____

_____

The Fall of Babylon

6. The judgments of Revelation are moral judgments. To what extent do you believe that we will be held accountable for our behavior?

_____

_____

_____

_____

_____

7. What evils that afflict you would you like to see destroyed?

_____

_____

_____

_____

_____

The Final Victory

In this life, no victories are final. No one is ever able to say, "That's it. Battle over. Now I can relax." Other enemies lie in wait. Other hurdles must yet be overcome. Life is an uphill pull all the way to the end.

The first readers of the Apocalypse knew this all too well. Pariahs in their own culture, objects of violent oppression and religious intolerance, they faced a constant struggle and a fierce opposition. Faith itself was a challenge, and faithfulness was an unending battle for survival.

It is to those Christians, as well as to struggling believers of every age, that the final chapters of Revelation are addressed. These chapters offer a story of a coming final victory. This victory will not have to be won again. It is the final victory, the final end of the last struggle. This is arguably the most sublime, hopeful, and empowering word ever written.

The Marriage Feast of the Lamb (Rev 19:5-10)

The story of the final victory begins in verse 5 with a doxology. At first, a single voice sings praise to God. Then, one verse later, a great multitude joins in, and together they sing their celebration that the long-awaited marriage feast of the Lamb has at last arrived. Obviously, the image of the supper is symbolic. The church could not be a literal bride, nor could it marry a literal Lamb. This is a celebration of a higher order. It is a celebration of the ultimate union of Christ and his followers. That, of course, is the final victory. George Beasley-Murray said in his commentary on Revelation that this passage does not tell us what the final victory is; it tells us what the final victory is like. The final victory is like a great marriage feast for Christ and his followers. That is, this banquet is so joyous, so magnificent, so amazing that it can only be likened to the most joyous of human occasions.

The bride at this wedding is of course the church, the full assembly of the redeemed. She is given "fine linen, bright and pure" (v. 8) to wear. The same church that is so flawed in her earthly incarnation is now dressed in the garments of purity. Her flaws were made clear in the letters to the seven churches. Christ even spoke of spewing one of those churches out of his mouth, so revolting were her evils. Now, however, something miraculous has happened. The bride has been made pure, her sins cleansed by the Lamb that was slain. Her shining garments are not the clothes she has worn on earth. They are given to her to wear. They are an act of grace by a God of mercy, and they symbolize the work of our redemption.

The groom, of course, is the Lamb. The imagery of the Lamb shifts through the pages of Revelation. When we first see him, he is a lion, but on second glance, he is a Lamb. The enemies of God slit his throat and murder him, but on yet another look he is a warrior, leading the conquerors into battle. Now, at the wedding supper, he is fully revealed as a bridegroom, wearing the many crowns of his victory. Never was a wedding as royal as this.

The fact that John's vision is couched in terms of a wedding is a powerful way of telling us that the relationship of Christ and the church is one of love. The bride has loved her groom, and though she has sometimes been unfaithful, she has followed him through the tribulation. The groom, by laying down his life for his bride, has blotted out the sins of the bride and dressed her in the wedding attire of perfect purity. If an angel were to intone the words of Paul recorded in Ephesians 5:25-26, it would surprise no one: "Christ loved the church, and gave himself up for her, in order to make her holy by cleansing her with the washing of water by the word."

This is a passage with a strong message for our day. The much discussed contemporary trend to be "spiritual but not religious" eliminates any real role for the church in the spirituality of our culture. The institutional church is seen as so flawed, so rigid, so political, so irrelevant to people's lives that instead of feeding the spirit, it quenches it. Before we get on that "trend train," we would do well to listen to Revelation. In John's apocalyptic vision, the same corrupted church we have known is dressed by the Lamb in the garb of purity. Her message may be shrouded in oppressive rules and rituals that have lost their meaning; she may live in moral hypocrisy, she may lapse into cultural irrelevancy, and she may perpetuate the hatreds and divisions of humanity, but she comes to wed the Lamb. She is, for all her failures, the bride of Christ.

Some may argue that this bride of Christ is the church universal, and not the flawed church on the corner. Revelation makes no such distinction. The seven churches with their ignoble flaws have in this vision become the triumphant church, and she stands in glowing white beside the Christ who has loved her. The church as seen in Revelation is both local and universal, both spirit and flesh, both temporal and eternal, both imperfect and redeemed. Christ died for the church local, the church cracked and fissured, the church impure and stained, not just the church purified. Otherwise, redemption is a farce. It is the tainted church that now stands so beautiful beside the Lamb. Her redemption is a key to the final victory. If we take her lightly in her impure incarnation on the earth, we do so at our peril.

At the end of the vision of the marriage feast, John falls overwhelmed at the feet of the angel who has unveiled it. The angel rebukes him in words that say essentially, "Don't do that! I am a fellow servant with you and with your brothers and sisters who hold to the testimony of Jesus. Worship only God!" Deliverers of bad news sometimes plead, "Please don't kill the messenger!" The angel here begs the opposite, basically saying, "Please don't worship the messenger. God has done this. He alone is worthy of your worship." The angel says that he is only a fellow servant. Those who deliver the message, whether angels or preachers, whether heavenly beings or Bible study leaders, are never worthy of our worship.

The Return of Christ (Rev 19:11-16)

Following the account of the marriage feast, Revelation finally gets to the subject for which most people read Revelation: the second coming. Oddly, perhaps, everything that Revelation says about the second coming is contained in six verses, and it does not contain the information that most readers have come to expect from popular "biblical" interpretations of the end times. Here, in capsule form, is all that Revelation says about the second coming: First, heaven stands open (just as it did at the baptism of Jesus), and a rider who is called Faithful and True appears on a white horse. After he appears, he judges with justice, wages war, has eyes like blazing fire, wears many crowns, has a name written on him that only he knows, wears a robe dipped in blood, and is also named the Word of God.

Following him are the armies of heaven, also riding on white horses and dressed in fine, white, clean linen. He carries only one weapon, a sword coming out of his mouth. With that sword he strikes down the nations that he will rule with an iron scepter. Finally, he treads the winepress of the wrath of God. Also, he has a name written on his robe and on his thigh "King of kings and Lord of lords" (v. 16).

That is literally all we are told. We can add a little information from a few other New Testament passages, but the Bible simply does not provide the detailed depiction for which we hunger and that misinterpretations have provided in such sensational fashion. These misinterpretations are, simply put, unbiblical, and they have been foisted onto an unsuspecting public and gone unchallenged for far too long. I believe that there are two reasons the Bible omits more specific details about the return of Christ: (1) We could not comprehend them if we had them. They describe a reality far, far larger than the usual picture we are given. (2) They would divert us from the message we are meant to hear. We would become so caught up in our fascination with the details that we would miss the message of hope that is at the heart of the second coming. We should not take the sacredness of Scripture so lightly as to read into the text more than is there. The truth is that we do not know when the second coming will occur, whether the skies will literally crack open, or whether Jesus will return on physical clouds. I believe the Bible teaches that the second coming is to be a spiritual event, and that its truth is most perceptible when it is heard not in rational human terms but in divine spiritual terms.

This approach, however, has allowed some to dismiss the second coming as simply the fantasy of a crazed prophet exiled on a rocky island in the Mediterranean. If we view Scripture as trustworthy, we are not free to do that. The parousia (as scholars call the second coming) is an important teaching in Scripture and must be taken seriously. What, then, can we affirm about the second coming that squares with Scripture?

First, we can affirm that, whatever it may be like, the Bible teaches that it will occur. The second coming is not found only in Revelation; it is found throughout the New Testament. In the Gospels, for example, Jesus himself tells of his return:

> "Then the sign of the Son of Man will appear in heaven, and then
> all the tribes of the earth will mourn, and they will see 'the Son
> of Man coming on the clouds of heaven' with power and great

glory. And he will send out his angels with a loud trumpet call, and they will gather his elect from the four winds, from one end of heaven to the other." (Matthew 24:30-31)

"Do not let your hearts be troubled. Believe in God, believe also in me. In my Father's house there are many dwelling places. If it were not so, would I have told you that I go to prepare a place for you? And if I go and prepare a place for you, I will come again and will take you to myself, so that where I am, there you may be also." (John 14:1-3)

This teaching is also clear in Paul's writings: "Then we who are alive and remain shall be caught up together with them in the clouds to meet the Lord in the air. And thus we shall always be with the Lord" (1 Thess 4:17). Furthermore, throughout its history the church has affirmed this teaching. The Nicene Creed, for example, which has been repeated weekly by many Christians since it was written in the fourth century, says this: "He [Jesus] will come again in glory to judge the living and the dead, and his kingdom will have no end. . . . We look for the resurrection of the dead, and the life of the world to come. Amen."

The biblical writers and the early Christians clearly believed that Jesus would return. These verses in Revelation were written to affirm them in that belief and to encourage them in their struggles against those who wanted to snuff out their movement at all costs. The fact of the parousia, and not any detailed account of its chronology and surrounding events, gave the early church the strength to survive. In fact, this was the message they assimilated into their lives: If persecution was coming, Christ was coming as well. If martyrdom awaited, Christ was coming to give them life. If the church stumbled and failed, Christ was coming to restore it. If human kings persecuted them, Christ was coming to establish his righteous reign. John's vision is not a revelation of graphic detail; it is a revelation of the final victory of God, and it allows the church in the meantime to affirm, "Christ has died, Christ is risen, Christ will come again!"

The second affirmation is already made, but let's highlight it before we move on. We can see the second coming only through a glass darkly, to use Paul's phrase from 1 Corinthians 13:12. Contrary to the first inclinations of human minds, faith does not require that we have a road map, a timetable, and a video trailer.

What it does require is hope. Revelation paints a hope-giving picture. It shows us a reality so large, so amazing, and so certain that it feeds the hope and empowers the action of the church. God will redeem the world through One so great that his thoughts are not our thoughts and his ways are not our ways, through One whose truths confound our little minds (Isa 55:8-9).

Third, we can affirm that the second coming calls us always to be prepared for the coming of God. The second coming means that justice is on the way. In the meantime, we must live our lives prepared for this, we must do our best to live according to his teachings, and we must accept and rely on God's grace. Preparedness allows us to anticipate his return eagerly and not to fear it. This is what allows Christians to persevere amid our present circumstances. How sad that, for many twenty-first century followers of Christ, the message of perseverance has been lost. In our time, great discouragement has gripped many churches. We are in need of the message of Revelation: persevere. As Jesus said, "The one who endures to the end will be saved" (Matt 10:22b). Christ is coming!

Fourth, we can affirm that most of the details we have from Revelation about the second coming are highly symbolic. A rider appears on a white horse, symbolizing the purity of its rider. (This is not the white horse from the four horsemen of the apocalypse in Rev 6:2.) This rider is the conquering Christ. His eyes blaze like fire, seeing all. His head bears many crowns, a physically difficult feat but a powerful reminder that this rider is King of all kings. His garment is dipped symbolically in the blood of his martyrs and in the blood of their redemption. His name is the Word of God, but he is also called Faithful and True, and written on his robe and his thigh is another name, King of kings and Lord of lords. These are not ordinary names, but they are names that, in the ancient tradition, reveal who he is. One more name is written on him, but this one does not reveal who he is, for only he knows this name. Only he can know the whole of his identity. The sword protruding from his mouth symbolizes that he will rule by the word of God. This is obviously a symbolic image, and to take it literally would take away from the majesty of this word from God.

Finally, we can affirm from this passage that Christ's return will be victorious. His return, in fact, not only proclaims his victory; it *is* his victory. Verse 15 says it clearly, using an Old Testament image that John also used in 2:27: "He will rule them with an iron scepter." In still another Old Testament image, John underscores

Christ's victory over evil: "He [Christ] treads the wine press of the fury of the wrath of God Almighty."

"Victory in Jesus" is an old gospel hymn, and as Christians have sung it they have pictured the victory in many ways. Revelation pictures it like this: Christ comes in victory accompanied by his soldiers who do not fight. They are his followers, and by the power of their witness and by the strength of his only weapon, the word of God, he rules not just individuals but "the nations." The power with which he will rule is so matchless that it is described in first-century terms as an iron scepter. He will crush the forces of evil and exalt the forces of God. He came the first time to be crucified. He comes the second time to reign.

The Last Battle (Rev 19:17-21)

This section has been dubbed "the last battle," but the label is a bit confusing. Is this the last battle, or was it Armageddon, or is it the attack of Gog and Magog that will come later? Or are they all the same battle, just pictured in different ways? Likely, they are just different pictures of the grand defeat of Satan at the end of time, but we cannot resolve this question with certainty.

In any event, the battle described here is a description not just of the beast and the false prophet but also of the cosmic force of evil behind them, the force we call the devil. The account of "the last battle" begins with another banquet that stands in stark contrast to the marriage feast of the Lamb. This banquet is a feast for the birds of the air. They dine on the flesh of kings and captains, mighty horses and riders, and the flesh of all, slave and free, small and great. The image is repulsive at first, but that changes when we see that the birds are feasting, in fact, on the carrion of evil. The consumption of the dead carcass of evil is a cause for rejoicing. This counter-banquet to the marriage feast repeats the theme John has heard so often as he has experienced his revelation: one day evil will fall, and even its corpse will be devoured. This is not just a gory description of buzzards eating human flesh. It is a picture of the final elimination of the evil that has corrupted human flesh.

The image of the feast of the birds is drawn from Ezekiel 39:17-20 and is, broadly speaking, the fulfillment of that prophecy. The Ezekiel account is slightly different: the beasts join the birds, and together they are invited to eat the flesh of the hosts of "Gog of Magog," which are apparently armies from the north that attack Israel after it is resurrected following the exile. In Revelation, Gog and Magog will shortly make an appearance, attacking the new Israel in the final days. The fact that the details of the two accounts do not match precisely does not matter. Revelation appropriates Ezekiel's symbol and expands it to demonstrate God's complete victory in the final battle.

Now the beast and the kings and (presumably) the false prophet gather with their armies to make war against the one named Faithful and True. No details of this battle are given, but the results are clear. The beast and the false prophet (the one who had deceived people into worshiping the image of the beast) are captured and thrown alive into the lake of fire. The rest are killed by the sword of the word of God, and on their flesh the birds continue their feast.

This lake of fire raises many questions for curious Bible readers. Is this lake of fire literal? Who burns in it? Where is it? To begin, the lake of fire is an image in Revelation for a place of eternal torment. It is a synonym for "Gehenna," the term used elsewhere in the New Testament. The word "Gehenna" was clearly derived from the name of the Valley of Hinnom, which lay outside the southern walls of the city of Jerusalem. Many readers will have heard that this valley was originally used to burn the garbage from the city, but George Beasley-Murray points out that the first mention of this idea is found in the writings of a Jewish scholar named Kimchi in about 1200. We know with greater certainty that the Valley of Hinnom in Old Testament times was a place of human sacrifice to the god Moloch. In either case, Gehenna symbolizes a place of suffering outside the city walls of the new Jerusalem. The fire probably represents spiritual suffering.

One thing is certain: being cast into the lake of fire does not mean extinction (see 20:10). The lake is a place of eternally tortured existence. After the last battle, the beast and the false prophet are cast into the lake to suffer forever. The rest, however, according to the Scripture, are killed. "The rest" does not mean all who reject God's grace; it means the rest of the armies led by the beast. They come to life again in John's vision when the "rest of the dead" (20:5) are raised following the millennium. This passage assures Christians that the forces that now inflict immeasurable suffering will be forever consumed by their own wickedness.

The Binding of Satan (Rev 20:1-3)

After the beast and the false prophet are cast into the lake of fire, God at last deals with that great enemy, the devil. Just to be sure that no one misses his identity, John calls him by several of his names: the dragon, that ancient serpent, the devil, Satan. In John's mind, this is the same prince of darkness who appeared earlier as the dragon, who tempted Adam and Eve in the Garden of Eden, who afflicted Job, and who has been known to human beings as the devil throughout all of time. When his time finally comes, God sends an angel who promptly dispatches the dragon to the lake of fire to suffer there with the beast and the false prophet, that is, with his own kind. As a kind of final insult, the destruction of the devil does not even require God's personal involvement.

John then sees the dragon cast into the Abyss, bound with a chain, and the Abyss itself sealed. The great demon can trouble God's followers no more. He is bound and sealed in the lake of fire for a thousand years.

Then comes one of the most enigmatic statements in the entire Apocalypse: "After that, he must be set free for a short time" (20:3b). This statement is a head turner. Why must Satan be set free again? If he has been defeated and the church has been delivered, and if God has the power to keep him chained, why would he be set free again?

These questions pose a problem only if we try to read this passage too literally. If we take the position that Revelation is not written to give us chronological details but to allow us to perceive the real meaning of the truth, then the release of Satan is more understandable. But what sense are we to make of it? We can best answer this as we consider what happens on earth during this thousand years of Satan's detention.

The Millennium (Rev 20:4-6)

If there were six verses telling us about the second coming, there are three that tell us about the millennium. These three verses provide all the biblical detail we have about this much-imagined time. The millennium of course is the thousand years in which John says that Christ will reign on earth before he establishes the new Jerusalem. Of course, many troubling questions arise. Why should there be a millennium? What is the purpose of Christ reigning a thousand years on earth? Why not just get on with the new Jerusalem? Why the delay when evil is defeated and Satan is bound? Why a thousand years? Why not five hundred? Why not a million? In order to put these questions in perspective, we need to understand the nature of the millennium as described by John.

What is the millennium? We have already said that it is a thousand-year reign of Christ on the earth, but like many other images in Revelation, the millennium has an Old Testament background. The feast of the birds was drawn specifically from Ezekiel 39:17-20, but this entire section of Revelation is inspired in part by Ezekiel 37–39. In those chapters, as we mentioned briefly above, Ezekiel tells of the reestablishment of the nation Israel after the Babylonian exile, an attack on Israel by "Gog of Magog" after an unspecified period, and finally the establishment of the new Jerusalem.

This same pattern occurs in Revelation, but John's vision adds new meaning to Ezekiel's prophecy. The unspecified period in Ezekiel becomes a thousand years in Revelation. The reestablishment of the new Israel in Revelation is not for an unspecified period but for a thousand years. "Gog of Magog" in Ezekiel becomes "Gog and Magog" in Revelation, mounting their attack not against Israel but against the new Israel. The end is not the reestablishment of an earthly new Jerusalem; it's a reestablishment of the eternal city.

The millennium itself is inserted into Ezekiel's unspecified period as a time in which evil is defeated and God's kingdom comes on earth. The evil that is defeated in the millennium is not cosmic evil or personal evil. It is social evil. The social order is replaced. The corrupt political and economic power of Babylon is crushed. When the power of Babylon is broken, Christ ushers in a golden millennium in which the earth is freed from the merciless conquerors of Babylon, the persecuting oppression of Rome, the greed of the rulers of the earth, the injustice of hunger, the suffering of the innocent, and the wars of all times. This is the message to John's audience: before the new Jerusalem comes, creation will pause to celebrate both the end of the social evils of this world and the glory of the one toward whom Isaiah pointed when he said, ". . . the government shall be upon his shoulder" (Isa 9:6, KJV).

Is the millennium, then, a literal thousand-year period? Personally, I do not think so. After all, why would this number be the only one in Revelation that is not symbolic? I believe that the number one thousand is a way of saying that Christ will have a long and glorious reign over a redeemed earth. In the final analysis, the length of the millennium should be no worry. It does not affect the central message of the millennium: that Christ will reign and the earth will be redeemed, that he cares not only for what happens in heaven but also for what happens here.

Why the millennium? Now comes what is perhaps the most puzzling question about the millennium. What is the point of a period of earthly glory when heaven is about to come? The answer is found in another question. Why would God extract his followers from a corrupted creation, take them to heaven, and then throw away what he has made? The millennium is an affirmation that God will not do this. He will not simply destroy the world in order to establish a more perfect world. He will redeem the world he has already made. Romans 8 also expresses this thought, telling us that "the creation itself will be set free from its bondage to decay and will obtain the freedom of the glory of the children of God" (Rom 8:21). In the millennium, creation is redeemed, and, as we saw above, so is the social order.

Who are the ones who reign with him? In the millennium, Christ is clearly supreme, but he does not reign alone. Verse 4 says that those who had not worshiped the beast reign with him. They sit on thrones, as pictured in Daniel 7:9, and have the authority to judge (that is, to rule). Those who have been martyred also reign with him (v. 4), having been brought back to life in what John terms the "the first resurrection" (v. 5). While Revelation does not refer to a "second resurrection" by name, the first resurrection is so called because "The rest of the dead did not come to life until the thousand years were ended" (v. 5a).

This has important meaning for the church. First, it means that the martyrs, those who have paid the highest price for the faith, will not only be saved but will also be exalted with Christ. Their vindication will occur not only in heaven but also before the eyes of the world. Second, it means that both martyrs and all struggling and suffering believers will one day reign with Christ and that, therefore, there is never a reason for them to give up, never a reason for them to grow weary, never a reason for them to surrender to Babylon. When Christ reigns supreme, all of his followers will be seated beside him. They will reign not in vengeance against their persecutors but in the spirit of millennium, an age when all things wrong are put right.

As spectacular as the millennial reign is, it is still an earthly reign. Death is still at work. The unredeemed still stir (otherwise, whom would the conquerors reign over?). The capacity for evil is still present. The new Jerusalem is yet to come.

When does/will the millennium occur? Those who read Revelation literally naturally ask when the millennium will come.

Prophecy, of course, never answers such questions. It impossible to predict a date for the millennium, perhaps because it does not occur in ordinary time. John does seem to expect it soon.

Even if Christians have been unsuccessful in establishing the date of the millennium, they have long debated its timing relative to other end-time events. Specifically, the debate has swirled around how the millennium is to be sequenced in relation to the second coming. The terms premillennial, postmillennial, and amillennial are at the center of this discussion. These terms are confusing to the average Christian, so here is a brief explanation of each.

Premillennialists believe that Christ will return before the millennium. Upon Christ's return, the dead in Christ shall rise and rule with him for a thousand years, but until that time the world will become increasingly evil. Only Christ's return will be sufficient to break the bonds of Satan and establish a golden messianic reign. One problem with this view is that it requires not only a second coming of Christ but also a third coming. This is because only the dead in Christ will have been raised at the second coming, and Christ will have to come yet again to raise everyone else for the final judgment. This is an event for which there is no clear evidence in Scripture. Premillennialism has been common in evangelical circles over the last century and a half, but this has not always been true of that group.

Postmillennialists believe that Christ will return after the millennium. The kingdom of God will extend its reach, more and more people will be converted, and the social order will get better and better until the millennium dawns. After this golden age, Christ will return and bring the new Jerusalem. Some readers are familiar with George W. Truett, a great evangelical preacher of the early twentieth century. Truett is a prime example of an evangelical postmillennialist. One of the problems with this view is that it is so overly optimistic that it takes its lumps anytime the world experiences major social catastrophes.

Amillennialists start from an entirely different premise. To be an amillennialist is to believe that the millennium began with Christ's first coming and will end with his second. In this view, "millennium" is a symbolic word that does not refer to a specific period. To amillennialists, the millennial reign exists alongside darkness, much as the wheat and the tares grow together in Jesus' parable.

The debate about these positions is endless, and we will not resolve them in this little book. There are positives and negatives to each point of view, but they seem to matter much more to us than they do to God. If the answer were clear in the Bible, this matter would have been settled long ago. Likely, our problem is that the whole discussion is based on an erroneous way of understanding Revelation. John's vision is not meant to reveal chronology or to describe literal events; it is meant to reveal visionary pictures of the end of time that will reveal enough truth to give us hope until the final day arrives and, by God's grace, we are able to see more clearly. Rather than answering questions born in a finite human framework, Revelation intends to affirm something far more important: that Christ will return, that he will destroy evil, and that he will establish his kingdom (Metzger, 95), both on earth and in the new Jerusalem.

The Defeat of Gog and Magog (Rev 20:7-10)

Someone once warned me that when you cut a snake's head off, it still wiggles a little. It turns out to be just so with the serpent that John calls the dragon. At the end of the millennium, he wiggles a little before his final demise. That is, he is set free again, albeit for a short time. His last spasm stirs up the nations of the earth, and he induces them to surround the encampment of God's people.

John calls the nations "Gog and Magog." Their identity has been much debated by the curious. Ezekiel refers to "Gog of Magog," Gog apparently being the ruler of a country called Magog. John, however, refers to Gog *and* Magog, apparently two countries. No one knows exactly how to account for this change. We do know that by John's time this term had come to represent the nations of the north, but John seems to see Gog and Magog as the nations of all the earth since he sees them coming from all four corners of the earth. If the interpretation of this passage depended on knowing the exact identity of Gog and Magog, we might be in trouble. Fortunately, this does not matter at all. The only thing that matters to our understanding is that they are evil nations that oppose God and his people. They rear their angry heads and hiss at the end of the millennium, but when they do they are crushed.

Though much feared by many who read the Apocalypse, Gog and Magog are spectacularly unsuccessful. Fire comes down from heaven and consumes them. After that, their master Satan is cast into the lake of fire to join the beast and the false prophet in eternal suffering. To John, eternal suffering is not off-putting in the least. It is good news. Evil, the great enemy of God, the great perpetrator of pain, the great slayer of human souls, will be stopped from his rampage and will suffer in immeasurable degree.

The lake of fire is probably not a literal lake of fire, since "Death" and "Hades" are cast into it. Neither of these are physical entities, so it is unlikely that the fiery lake would be. Even if the lake is not literal, however, it is real. Its pain may be fiercer than literal flames could be. This much we know for sure: when Satan takes up residence there, he will trouble God's people no more. All will be ready for the arrival of the new Jerusalem.

The Last Judgment (Rev 20:11-15)

The last of John's seven visions of the end reveals a great white throne and the "one who was seated on it" (v. 11). The throne is a throne of judgment, and the one seated on it is Christ in his full divinity. Father and Son have become one on this throne. The perfect judge and the perfect redeemer come in one person to judge the world. This judgment will not be executed imperfectly as by human judges, but perfectly by the Lord of lords.

The dead stand before the throne, but what dead are they? Are they only those who were not raised at the beginning of the millennium, or do they include those who ruled with Christ for a thousand years? Answering this question forces the discussion into a degree of specificity that I believe John never intended. John saw a dream-like picture intended to convey meaning deeper than the obvious. It was not a revelation of the physical details of the end time; it was something far more important. Even so, only one formal judgment scene occurs in Revelation, and it is the great white throne judgment. God's people are not exempt. Revelation 20:12 makes clear that even those whose names are written in the book of life are judged at the last day. Accountability is universal.

As the judgment unfolds before John's eyes, he says that "books were opened" (v. 12). There are two books involved. The first is a book of deeds, a record of the behavior of each person much like the records Persian kings kept on their subjects. Human actions are about to be judged, but still there is hope. Unlike the Persian kings, God keeps two books. The second book John describes is the Lamb's book of life that lists the names of all those whom the Lamb claims as his own. These are followers of God who acknowledge their own inadequacy and accept the Lamb's redemptive sacrifice in place of their own failed righteousness. It is important to note that, in the great white throne judgment, both deeds and faith shape our fate, but the sacrifice of the Lamb, the grace of God, is the final determinant. Those who have not availed themselves of God's grace, whose names are not written in the Lamb's book of life, are cast into the lake of fire.

If then, the grace of God is finally determinant, why is there a book of deeds at all? This raises the age-old question of whether we are saved by faith or works, and about all we can say for certain is this: faith is the key to eternal life, but it can only be used when we recognize the failure of our deeds. The road to eternal life is not simply to believe the right things, to join the right church, or to express faith in the right words. It is to seek to do good with all our might and then, when we have failed, to avail ourselves of the grace of God. Only those who deny themselves this grace will die in their sins. Both books are opened at the judgment. Both books matter.

John does not leave this subject without affirming strongly once more that no one escapes the judgment. Everyone must at last face God. In John's vision, even the sea gives up its dead for the judgment. Many people in John's day believed that those buried in the sea would be separated from their loved ones in the afterlife (Beasley-Murray, 302). Revelation affirms that even these will be present for judgment along with Death and Hades. Finally, he asserts "...all were judged according to what they had done" (v. 13).

The message given to John is clear: all people are accountable for the way they use their lives. Even Caesar in all his splendor will stand before God, and there he will recognize the one who is really Lord of all. The persecutors of the church will stand to give an account to the church's Master. Ordinary people who have lived simple lives will stand in the searing light of judgment, discovering there that even though they thought their lives and deeds did not matter, they were important to God. We who count ourselves as God's redeemed shall stand with them, as guilty perhaps as all the others, but declared innocent by the power of the Lamb. Hell, after all, is real. Judgment is real. An end is coming in which the only victory is the one to be found in the life-giving Lamb that was slain. By means of his sacrificial love, the new heaven and the new earth will be established.

1. Who are the "bride" and the "groom" at the wedding feast of the Lamb? Why would images of a wedding be chosen?

_____

_____

_____

_____

_____

2. What misunderstandings of the second coming have you encountered?

_____

_____

_____

_____

_____

3. What does the second coming of Jesus mean for believers?

_____

_____

_____

_____

_____

4. What is the meaning of the birds feasting on the flesh of those defeated in the final battle?

_____

_____

_____

_____

_____

5. Why is Satan bound during the millennium if he is only going to be released again before the coming of the new Jerusalem?

_____
_____
_____
_____
_____

6. Why is there a millennial reign? Once having defeated Satan, why does God not skip right to the new Jerusalem?

_____
_____
_____
_____
_____

7. What is the meaning of Gog and Magog? Why must they arise in John's vision?

_____
_____
_____
_____
_____

8. What are the two books at the last judgment, and how are they related to one another?

_____
_____
_____
_____
_____

The Last of the Last Things

Revelation 21–22

Finish, then, Thy new creation;
Pure and spotless let us be.
Let us see Thy great salvation
Perfectly restored in Thee;
Changed from glory into glory,
Till in heaven we take our place,
Till we cast our crowns before Thee,
Lost in wonder, love, and praise.
—"Love Divine, All Loves Excelling" (Charles Wesley, 1747)

The first summer we were married, my wife and I saw a Broadway play that helped in some ways to shape my theology. It was the musical play known as *Purlie*, the story of an African-American preacher who returns to his hometown in Jim Crow Georgia to open a church. He wants to purchase the old Big Bethel Church building to house his church, but Ol' Cap'n, the white patriarch of the community, tries to block Purlie's purchase at every turn. Near the end of the play, Ol' Cap'n's son Charlie finally helps Purlie and his followers to acquire the building. When Purlie and his followers realize that the building is theirs, their spirits soar, and in solidarity with them Charlie bursts into song: "The world ain't comin' to an end, my friend, The world is comin' to a start! I feel it in my heart. The world is comin' to a start."

Sitting in that crowded New York theater all those years ago, it dawned on me that Charlie's message is strongly akin to what John is conveying to us in the last two chapters of Revelation. John turns to his final vision fully aware that all the judgments he has described have led to the grand unveiling now before him. Here at last is seen the final destiny of God's creation. The first eighteen chapters were prologue: the incisive letters to the churches, the painful descriptions of the tribulations past and the great tribulation that awaits, the fearsome battles with Satan and his evil forces, the terrible pictures of the judgments of God. These lead finally to a sublime picture of the new creation. This vision is the primary revelation John was summoned to see. This vision motivated his writing and has inspired the greatest poets, preachers, and musicians of history. This is the vision that has given centuries of struggling believers the power to persevere. Robert Frost once speculated in a poem about whether the world would end in fire or ice. John's answer is, "Neither. It ends in a new creation." The end is not doom but glory, not bad news but good.

"Finish, Then, Thy New Creation" (Rev 21:1-8)

John opens the final section of the Apocalypse with the boldest of claims: "Then I saw a new heaven and a new earth . . ." (21:1a). John is reporting a new miracle of creation that is nothing short of the original. The first creation birthed billions of galaxies with whirling stars, black holes, dark matter, revolving planets, and one earth (as far as we know) with land, sea, sky, plants, animals, night, day, and human beings. A greater miracle now appears to John. He saw an entirely new creation, and it was of an order infinitely higher than the old one. For eighteen chapters, John told us how badly the old creation has gone awry. It was defiled, corrupted, and twisted out of its original beauty. Now it has passed away under the sentence of God, so that he might start all over again and create a new heaven and a new earth. Do not let the simple words fool you: the claim is astounding.

I once heard a preacher deal with the question of whether the new heaven and the new earth would be totally new or just renovated versions of the creation we already know. John's words leave no room for debate: ". . . the first heaven and the first earth had passed away" (21:1b). This, however, is not what the passage is about. John did not write these words to tell us how God created the new order. He wrote them to tell us of the incomparable majesty of God's new work of creation.

Revelation describes only one location in the new creation, namely, the new Jerusalem. She appears as "a bride adorned for her husband," a bride ready for the marriage feast of the Lamb. At the marriage feast in chapter 19, the bride was the church. Here in chapter 21, the bride is also the church, for the redeemed church is what the new Jerusalem is.

In the new Jerusalem, John says, there will be no more sea. This is curious. For the whole of history, many people have chosen to live relatively close to an ocean. Why should heaven have no sea? Is the point that its inhabitants should be deprived of beaches and sea breezes? No, the point is that dwellers in the new Jerusalem will suffer neither the danger that comes from the sea nor the separation that it causes.

Some wonder whether the fact that Revelation 4:6 mentions "something like a sea of glass" in heaven means that there is a contradiction here. Is there a sea, or is there not a sea? If we see both passages as describing spiritual and not physical realities, the apparent contradiction no longer matters. The glassy sea in chapter 4 makes a spiritual point; the absence of a sea in chapter 21 makes a spiritual point; and both of these points are valid. As long as we try to understand John's vision in literal terms, we will never understand the book of Revelation.

The new Jerusalem comes down out of heaven. It has no human origin. It is not the Jerusalem of Israel rebuilt. It is rather a new creation, only possible because of the intentional creative activity of God. This is the city of God. Its light is his glory. Its air is his presence. Unlike every other city, it is sent to us. We could never build it.

John's description of what life will be like in this heavenly city is one of the most moving passages in all of literature. In the New Revised Standard Version, verse 4 reads, ". . . he will wipe every tear from their eyes. Death will be no more; mourning and crying and pain will be no more, for the first things have passed away." As is often the case, John's vision is inspired by the prophets. Much of the language in this verse is also found Isaiah 25:6-8.

The promise goes on: "See, I am making all things new" (v. 5). He does not promise to mend his creation, cleanse it, or refinish it; he promises to make it new. Newness is always a wonder. It implies a state of perfection. The new suit has a perfect finish and a perfect fit. The new car has a perfect body and parts that all work. The new baby is born in perfect innocence, often with perfect skin. God promises to make all things new, that is, to make them whole and beautiful and pure, to give them a future after their future was lost.

Newness is also a word we use to describe what we have not yet experienced. Part of the reason the new creation defies ordinary forms of description is that it is filled with what we have never experienced before. Nevertheless, we are among those things that are made new, and so we shall be at home in the new creation. We can hardly imagine ourselves in the new creation, for we will be re-created into something for which we have potential even now, but have not yet experienced.

The words of this promise, God tells us, are faithful and true (v. 5). This affirmation is to reassure readers to whom the promise seemed incredible. To them, God says, "Trust me. I will wipe every tear from your eyes. I will take away your pain. I will conquer death." Only here in all of Revelation does God himself speak directly.

It is striking that God says, "I am making all things new" (v. 5). That is, he is not waiting until the end of time to start his new creation; he is already on task. While many Christians of John's day are experiencing persecution and death, God is making all things new. While old enmities are disrupting the world, God is making all things new. While our old bodies are decaying, God is making all things new. God does not announce from the future that he is now beginning his new creation. Rather, he says, "It is done!" These words were enough to give strength to the first-century church, and they are enough to give strength to the twenty-first-century church. When all our trials are over, as the hymn says, God will "finish, then," his new creation.

At the end of the age the heavenly city descends, and at the end of the age the one seated on the throne says to John, "It is done!" (v. 6). Jesus had said in John 14:3 that he would go and prepare a place for us. Now he has completed his preparation. The end has come, and the voice from the throne reminds John that he need not fear. He, God, was the beginning, and he is the end: "I am the Alpha and the Omega, the beginning and the end" (v. 6). G. B. Caird put it well when he wrote that the end is a person, not an event (266). Revelation reveals Christ and not chronology, as we have so often believed.

Who are the inhabitants of this new creation? They are the conquerors, John says (v. 7). Have they then earned their way into the holy city? This is a strange idea to those of us steeped in the belief that salvation is a free gift of God and that we can do nothing to earn it ourselves. John buys in to this to a point. When he depicted the conquerors in chapter 19, they conquered not by fighting but by standing by the victorious Lamb. Still, John does not back away from affirming that we play a role in our salvation. The inheritors of the kingdom are those who have endured the tribulation, who have risen above the affliction, who have resisted temptation, and who have joined with the Lamb as he has conquered evil. Salvation, as John understands it, requires believers to oppose evil wherever we find it. Defeating hunger and poverty, conquering corruption in business and government and churches, disarming those who oppress the weak, renouncing greed, and resisting temptation are all contributions to the saving work God does as he crushes evil. These victories are possible only through the Lamb that was slain, but we are his partners in the struggle. Being advocates of righteousness and conquerors of evil prepares us for the kingdom. James says it this way: "So faith by itself, if it has no works, is dead" (Jas 2:17).

At the same time, John says that those who fail to conquer and who live in opposition to God will have no part in the new creation (v. 8). Obviously, this means that John does not believe that God will save everyone in the end. For him, evil is real. He has seen the dragon and his beasts. He has experienced the sting of evil. He knows that evil should be taken seriously because it has the power to destroy.

"Pure and Spotless Let It Be" (Rev 21:9–22:5)

Then one of the angels who had delivered the seven bowls took John to "a great, high mountain" and showed him the holy city "coming down out of heaven from God" (v. 10). The description of that city is one of the most beautiful in all of literature. The entire Apocalypse has led to this supreme vision. That one of the angels of judgment shows him the city is no accident, because the angel's deliverance of judgment was necessary to prepare the way for the shining city. Judgment is the dark background against which the new Jerusalem stands in bold relief. Its coming is a surprise, for even while John is still absorbing what he has seen, the city is already coming down in grace.

The new Jerusalem has some of the attributes of the earthly Jerusalem. For example, the new Jerusalem has a wall around it just like ancient cities did, although we can hardly imagine its purpose in heaven. In its wall are gates, just as was necessary in the city wall of the old Jerusalem. These gates allow the kings of the earth "to bring their glory into" the city, although we might wonder why the kings of the earth are still permitted entrance, especially since their realms have passed away. (Zechariah 2:5 says that the restored

Jerusalem will need no wall, another indication that this wall is not to be understood as a literal wall. These seemingly contradictory statements are both valid because each speaks symbolically of different attributes of the city.) Such earthly attributes of the heavenly city might give us pause. Some interpreters have suggested that the new Jerusalem looks a lot like the earthly Jerusalem because John sees it during the millennium. Others think that some marks of the old Jerusalem are still present as an indication that the kingdom of God will finally come on earth, just as Jesus asked in the Lord's Prayer. For my part, I think that the similarities of the new Jerusalem to the old are present because John and his readers cannot imagine it any other way. We must be able to link the heavenly city to the only reality we know, or we can never begin to grasp it. As Paul wrote, citing Isaiah 64:45, "What no eye has seen, nor ear heard, nor the human heart conceived, what God has prepared for those who love him" (1 Cor 2:9).

These two examples of earthly features in John's description are best understood as pictures suggesting a larger reality. The wall is obviously not for defense; the wars against evil are over. Rather, the walls mark a geography of the spirit and serve as a reminder that those who dwell in that city are safe forever. The kings are said to enter the city as a way of demonstrating that God has now established his sovereignty over all. Even the faded glory of earthly kings is laid at the feet of God (v. 25).

The size of the city is stated in specific earthly dimensions: It is 1,500 miles cubed. These measurements, however, are not intended to depict the literal size of the heavenly city. Instead, they are intended to convey the enormity of the city. God's eternal city is unimaginably big. It will have room for all those who follow him. The old hymn, "There's Room at the Cross for You," makes the same point John makes as he reports the dimensions of heaven.

If the city is said to be a cube, this statement has a spiritual point. In the Jerusalem temple, the holy of holies was shaped like a cube (1 Kgs 6:20). This was so because, in the ancient world, people regarded the cube as a perfect shape. The city of God, Revelation is saying, is perfect in all its dimensions. Nothing in it is flawed, nothing in it is wanting, nothing in it is blemished. Even its wall is perfect, measuring 144 cubits, the number (12 times 12) that stands for perfection squared. (Incidentally, if these numbers are to be taken literally, we will be hard pressed to understand why a 1,500-mile-high city has a wall only 216 feet high.)

Another spiritual point is made as John describes the composition of the city and its wall. The wall is made of jasper and the city is pure gold (v. 18). In verse 11, jasper was the image that showed how the city radiated the presence of God, and so it would follow that here in verse 18, jasper means that even the walls radiated his presence. When we speak of anything we value highly, we often say it is pure gold. That is what John says of the city he saw. His clear meaning is that this city is to be valued more than all other treasures.

The description goes further. The twelve foundations of the walls are adorned with precious stones. The gates are each made of giant pearl. The street is pure gold. (Once I heard a preacher make the point that Revelation does not say that the streets of heaven are paved with gold but that they *are* pure gold. To this day, I have not been able to understand the difference between the two, but I have concluded that it is not a matter for concern.) The jewels, the pearls, and the gold are powerful ways of conveying the beauty, the majesty, and the incomparable value of the eternal city.

John then takes note of several things that are not in the city. First, there is no temple, for God himself is the temple (v. 22). That is, the city itself is sacred space, so there is no need of any special sacred space within it. Every inch of the new Jerusalem is shot through with the glory of God. But didn't chapter 15 speak of a temple in heaven? In Revelation 15:5, there is a reference to "the temple of the tent of witness in heaven." Is the absence of a temple in chapter 21 a contradiction? Several explanations are possible. Chapter 15 could represent heaven before the return of Christ and chapter 21 afterward. Or we could say that heaven in chapter 15 is a different reality from the new creation in chapter 21. Neither of these answers is satisfying to me. The better explanation might be that John is continuing to speak in the rich and truthful language of symbols. The "temple of the tent of witness" in chapter 15 is a reminder that the God who camped with wandering Israel will be encamped eternally among those who dwell in heaven. The city without a temple in chapter 21 is a reminder of the abiding presence of God in the new Jerusalem.

No sun or moon shines over this city, for its light is God. The Lamb, the passage says, is his lamp. Isaiah 9:2 said that those who walk in darkness have seen a great light. Here in the new Jerusalem, his prophecy has come to pass: the children of light are finally at home.

Three more characteristics are mentioned: the gates of the new Jerusalem will never be shut (v. 25), night will never fall there (v. 25), and the unclean will never enter its precincts (v. 27). All three characteristics are taken directly from description of the restored temple in Isaiah 60.

All the attributes of the new Jerusalem add up to one simple fact: this is the place of grace, the eternal dwelling place where mortals put on the mantle of immortality, and where the children of God dwell in intimate nearness to the heart of God. A few final images reinforce John's understanding that this city is a place of perfect blessedness.

The angel shows him the river of life that flows by the tree of life. In the Garden of Eden, there was a river and a tree of life. Are these the same? That is an unanswerable question, but they are images that intentionally link the new creation story to the old. Certainly, the tree and the river at the end of time are something more than they were in the garden. They show that God intended to give this kind of life in the beginning and that he has not been thwarted in his desire. At the end of history, the river and the tree are still there, and the life God gives through them pulsates in the new creation. The river and the tree are again spiritual realities. The tree grows and the river flows wherever God bestows life.

Strikingly, creation is book-ended by the tree and the river, that is, by the gift of life. In the Epistle of Barnabas, an early Christian document not in the Bible, God says, "Behold, I make the last things as the first" (Barnabas 6:13). As it turns out in Revelation, however, the last things are even greater than the first. This time there will be no serpent, no temptation, no fall. There will only be the gift of life and the One who gives it.

The water of the river is the water of life, which is also mentioned in John's Gospel. This water nourishes the tree of life, which grows on both sides of the river. The tree yields twelve kinds of fruit, a different one for each month of the year, leaving no gap in God's provision for his faithful. The leaves of the tree contain healing for the nations. Wounds and divisions that have long festered are made whole by the leaves. The tree and the river are God's never-ending source of life, and so life in the great city is unending and abundant. They are also God's never-ending sources of peace, and so life in the great city will be marked by the peace for which all people yearn so deeply.

In that city are also the throne of God and the Lamb. This means that God's followers dwell in his court, the court of the King of kings. They are exalted from their low status. They are now living the nobility of the kingdom of God. There in the courts of God, they are able to see his face in an intimacy no one has experienced before, not even Moses (Exod 33:20). Those who seek his face at last shall find it. The lowly, as Mary sang in her Magnificat, have been lifted up (Luke 1:52).

Paul had said that in this world we see in part and we know in part (1 Cor 13:9). That is, we see only part of God, only part of truth, only part of the glory that is to be revealed. How could it be otherwise? Our vision is too small, our minds too slow, our hearts too hardened, our spiritual vision too dim. In the new creation, however, we shall at last see him face to face, for he will have drawn so near that even we can see him.

The angel also shows John that God's name is written on the forehead of every believer. That name has protected them in times of tribulation; now it identifies them in eternity. They have finally become who they truly are: the people of God. Some people wear their religion on their sleeves for show. In the new creation, God's children will wear their religion on their foreheads as a sign of their identity. When worn on our sleeves, religion is often a sign of who we want others to think we are or, worse, of the power it gives us over others. When worn on our foreheads, however, the name of God is written into our flesh; it announces our uniqueness in an unmistakable way.

Those who wear the mark are unimaginably blessed, and it is said that they will reign "forever and ever" (22:5). But over whom will they reign? Possibly, they could reign over each other, but that would make no sense since they all reign together. Or they could reign over those suffering in the lake of fire, but that hardly seems likely, especially since it is not mentioned anywhere else. Perhaps they reign over themselves. That might be closer to the mark, since all those who live in the new city failed to reign over themselves in their lives on earth. That is precisely why they needed to be redeemed. Or maybe they will reign over the unseen realms that lie beyond the universe and beyond the reality that is knowable in this life. Most likely, however, this statement has nothing to do with whom they shall reign over. Instead, it is a statement that affirms their nobility, recognizing their coronation with the glory and grace and royalty of God. They have been tapped with the sword of his word and so exalted in his kingdom. They rule not as monarchs in their own right but as grace-baptized participants in the sovereign glory of God.

"Till We Cast Our Crowns before Thee" (Rev 22:6-21)

The vision is now coming to an end, as visions always do. The recipients of John's letter must go back to living under the yoke of oppression and the threat of persecution. They must go back to churches where would-be followers of God squabble and forget their purpose. The people of God must await the promised glory while living in an inglorious world. Verses 6-21 form the epilogue to the book of Revelation, and in them John offers believers what they need to live in the dismal meantime. Highlighting the central points of the revelation he has received, he holds out to his readers a bright and certain hope. In these closing verses, John offers a final promise, some final instructions, a final warning, a final reassurance, a final plea, and a final blessing.

The final promise is that he is coming soon. This promise, like the others, John tells us, can be depended on because the revelation given to him is "faithful and true." After all, God himself sent an angel to reveal it (v. 6). Believers in distress who especially need the knowledge that Christ is coming soon could not divine it by reason, so God revealed it to them. Some thinkers believe that truth is available only through reason. There is no way to prove or disprove this statement. People of faith believe that there is a reality that cannot be known by our senses and measured with our instruments. It can only be known as it is revealed to us. This statement cannot be proved or disproved either. Christians, however, believe that the capacity of the human mind is limited, and that human beings are not gods. For me, that tilts the balance. Revelation is not just wishful thinking; it is real.

The word "soon" perplexed us before, and now it perplexes us again. He is coming soon, Jesus says, but soon by whose definition? Soon is one thing to a four-year-old and another to a centenarian. What must it mean to God? Many of the early Christians believed that this meant Jesus would return in their lifetimes, but we must remember that this is the voice of God speaking. He uses the word "soon" from his perspective and not from ours. We will never resolve exactly what "soon" means when Jesus says, " I am coming soon," but we are sure of this: the word "soon" is the response of God to believers who suffer tribulation and ask, "How long, O Lord?" His answer might be paraphrased, "Not forever, my child. Not forever."

The final promise is followed immediately with final instructions for the meantime. "Here's what's coming" is followed by "here's how you wait for it." Before looking at the instructions themselves, ponder for a moment John's preface to the final instructions: a statement that anyone who keeps "the words of the prophecy of this book" will be blessed (v. 7b). This warning demands to be taken seriously, so let's ask what it means to "keep" words of prophecy. If the words of Revelation are only a prediction of the events of the end time, then the instruction to keep them means nothing more than to hold on to them as a hope. But prophecy is, and always has been, much more than prediction. As we discussed earlier in this book, prophecy is about judgment and hope, so that the instruction to keep the words of this prophecy has an ethical meaning for those who live their lives before the final days. In other words, the prophecy of Revelation says, "Rulers, stop persecuting my people. Christians, be faithful to the life you have chosen. Lukewarm followers, heat your hearts and be ready. Evildoers, turn your lives around and do good. Churches, remember what you were created for in the first place. You who are persecuted, be comforted, have hope." Heard in this way, the message here is a kind of summary of the admonitions that were given to the seven churches. Revelation is prophecy in its highest sense: an invitation to obedience, a summons to action, a charge to righteousness, a call for repentance.

Now come the instructions. Here is a list, with a brief word about each:

1. Do not worship the messenger (vv. 8-9). For the second time, an angel rebukes John for worshiping him instead of God. The angel's message is clear: "Only God is worthy of worship. This is the second time I've told you. Stop worshiping the messenger. Got it now?" This is a message ultimately for us all.

2. Do not seal up the words of this book, "for the time is near" (v. 10). Daniel (along with Enoch, in a book not in the Bible) was told to seal the words he had written, for they were for another time. The angel (or is it the Lamb?) tells John that the time for such words has come. John has been charged to deliver his message now; it is urgent.

3. Remember that justice will be done in the end. That is the meaning of the strange words, "Let the evildoer still do evil, . . . and the holy still be holy" (v. 10). Some have thought this instruction means that the time for repentance is over, but verses 14 and 17 issue clear calls to repentance, so this cannot be the case. Rather, the meaning of these words is reminiscent of Jesus' parable of the weeds growing up beside the wheat (Matt 13:24-30). The message is something like this: "Do not fret too much about evil. God will sort everything out in the end. He will repay everyone for what they have done. He is, after all, the Alpha and the Omega."

4. Repent. Those who wash their robes, or repent, may enter the city gates and feast on the fruit of the tree of life (v. 14). Repentance does not mean simply being sorry for the wrongs we have done. It means turning our lives around. Repentance is a leaving behind and a becoming. It is a metamorphosis. Those who never "morph" by God's grace into new creations will surely dwell outside the city.

Christ authenticates these instructions by assuring John's readers that he is the one who sent the revelation (v. 16). He reminds us that he is the descendant of David, so we can know that this revelation is consistent with all previous revelations to Israel. Christ also says that he is "the bright and morning star," echoing Numbers 24:17: ". . . a star shall come out of Jacob, and a scepter shall rise out of Israel . . . ." Now this bright and morning star has brought the promise of a new age, a new city, a new creation, and a certain hope that it is drawing near.

Therefore Jesus offers an invitation to those who have not yet been grasped by the hope of the revelation: "The Spirit and the bride say, 'Come'" (v. 17a). This is a wedding invitation to the marriage of the Lamb. To those who have already been grasped by this hope he offers a separate invitation to share with the world: ". . . let everyone who hears say, 'Come'" (v. 17b). In beautiful words inspired by Isaiah 55:1, the Lamb invites all who are thirsty to come and drink from the waters of the river of life. These words, many readers will remember, inspired the lyrics of a gospel hymn: "Shall we gather at the river, that flows by the throne of God?"

After the final instructions comes a final warning: do not tamper with this message (vv. 18-19). Tampering with documents to change their message was a common practice in the ancient world. Since books were copied by hand, it was easy to alter them to mean something different from their authors intended. In fact, some other early Christian writings had already been altered in this way. Because of this kind of corruption of many books, many writings (for at least 2,500 years) included such prohibitions (Beasley-Murray, 346).

Of course, books are now printed and not hand-copied, so they are not so easily vulnerable to unethical editing. Or are they? When we reduce the sacred poetic language of Revelation to coded statements about the chronology of the end of time, have we not taken away from the words of Revelation? When we read various teachings into Revelation that are not there (the rapture, for instance), have we not added to the words of Revelation? The revelation John received is an important word offered to strengthen a church under assault from the forces of evil. Its message must get through without being corrupted. (That, more than any other reason, is why I wanted to write this book.)

The final reassurance is a repetition of the final promise. He is coming soon (v. 20). Reassurances often must be offered more than once. Anxious people find too many reasons to doubt them. They sound too good to be true, and as a result they are easily dismissed. The repetition of reassurances, then, is itself reassuring.

The final plea is a response to Christ's promise to come soon: "Amen. Come, Lord Jesus" (v. 20)! Twenty-first-century believers, like first-century believers, live in a fallen world where the evils of the age obscure the light of God, where faith is mocked, where the blood of war flows, where the poor too often starve, where greed is god, where hatred is rife, where hearts are so deeply broken that healing scarcely seems possible, where goodness fails, and where evil is all too often in the ascendancy. John's plea is as relevant to us as it was to first-century believers: "Come, Lord Jesus! Come in judgment over all that is evil. Come in grace over all those who hunger for your presence. Come in the light of glory to those of us who walk beneath the dark clouds of hopelessness. Come, Lord Jesus!"

And then the letter ends. It ends with a final blessing, not a final curse: "The grace of the Lord Jesus be with all the saints. Amen" (v. 21). This is the final word of Revelation and the final word in the Bible, a blessing of grace for those who wait. This is the amazing grace of Christ, the truest foretaste of the glory for which we hope.

1. What does it mean that the new Jerusalem "comes down" from heaven?

_____

_____

_____

_____

_____

2. How do you understand the absence of a sea and a temple in the new Jerusalem?

_____

_____

_____

_____

_____

3. Can you remember an experience in which life around you seemed new? How can that experience teach you about God's statement, "Behold, I am making all things new"?

_____

_____

_____

_____

_____

4. What do you make of the fact that the new Jerusalem has some earthly attributes?

_____

_____

_____

_____

5. Can you name some of the characteristics of the new Jerusalem as John saw it?

_____

_____

_____

_____

_____

6. Jesus said he was coming soon. What do you think he meant?

_____

_____

_____

_____

_____

7. Do you think that tampering with Revelation is still a temptation today? Why or why not?

_____

_____

_____

_____

_____

8. List some of the instructions God gives us for living as we wait for the new creation.

_____

_____

_____

_____

_____

Bibliography

Aune, David E. *Word Biblical Commentary: Revelation 1–5*. Dallas: Word Books, 1997.

———. *Word Biblical Commentary: Revelation 6–16*. Nashville: Thomas Nelson Publishers, 1998.

Aune, David E. *Word Biblical Commentary: Revelation 17–22*. Nashville: Thomas Nelson Publishers, 1998.

Beasley-Murray, George R. *The New Century Bible Commentary: Revelation*. Grand Rapids MI: William B. Eerdman's Publishing Company, 1974.

Blevins, James L. *Revelation as Drama*. Nashville: Broadman Press, 1984.

Boring, M. Eugene. *Interpretation: Revelation*. Louisville: John Knox Press, 1989.

Caird, G. B. *The Revelation of St. John the Divine*. London: Adam and Charles Black, 1966.

Draper, James T., Jr. *The Unveiling*. Nashville: Broadman Press, 1984.

Eliot, T. S. "The Hollow Men," 1925.

Ford, J. Massyngberde. *The Anchor Bible: Revelation*. New York: Doubleday Dell Publishing Group, 1975.

Greene, Oliver B. *Revelation*. Greenville: The Gospel Hour, 1963.

Hays, Richard B. *The Moral Vision of the New Testament*. San Francisco: Harper Collins, 1996.

Interpreter's Bible, volume 12, Nashville: Abingdon Press, 1957.

Keats, John. "Ode on a Grecian Urn" (from Arthur Quiller-Couch, ed., *The Oxford Book of English Verse: 1250–1900*, 1919). Bartleby.com, http://www.bartleby.com/101/625.html (accessed 23 October 2013).

Ladd, George Eldon. *The Blessed Hope*. Grand Rapids MI: William B. Eerdman's Publishing Company, 1956.

————. *A Commentary on the Revelation of John*. Grand Rapids MI: William B. Eerdman's Publishing Company, 1972,

LaHaye, Tim, and Jerry B. Jenkins, *Left Behind*. Carol Stream: Tyndale House Publishers, 1995.

Lindsey, Hal. *The Late Great Planet Earth*. Grand Rapids MI: Zondervan, 1970.

Metzger, Bruce M. *Breaking the Code*. Nashville: Abingdon Press, 1993.

Mounce, Robert H. *The New International Commentary: The Book of Revelation* (*NIC*), revised. Grand Rapids MI: William B. Eerdman's Publishing Company, 1977.

————. *What Are We Waiting For?* Grand Rapids MI: William B. Eerdman's Publishing Company, 1992.

Pagels, Elaine. *Revelations*. New York: Viking, 2012.

Reddish, Mitchell G. *Smyth & Helwys Bible Commentary: Revelation*. Macon: Smyth & Helwys, 2001.

Rossing, Barbara R. *The Rapture Exposed*. Boulder CO: Westview Press, 2004.

Schüssler Fiorenza, Elisabeth. *The Book of Revelation: Justice and Judgment*, 2nd ed. Minneapolis: Fortress Press, 1998.

Witherington, Ben, III. *Revelation and the End Times*. Nashville: Abingdon Press, 2010.

Wright, N. T. *Revelation for Everyone*. Louisville: Westminster John Knox Press, 2011.

Study the Bible ...

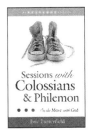
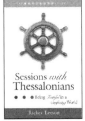

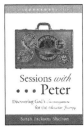